Praise for *How to Get a J* T0277236

'Incredibly practical guidance and tips from John Lees. While grounded in today's market context, the advice is timeless.'
Peter Yarrow, Global Head of Learning, Aberdeen

'These days it's easy to find a job but it's much harder to find a job you love. Packed with practical exercises, this timely book will help you choose wisely whether you're starting out or starting over again.'
Jacqueline Davies, NHS Director of Leadership, Talent and Lifelong Learning (MD, The NHS Leadership Academy)

'I am delighted to recommend this latest edition. I have used John's advice myself over the years and find it a wonderful source of guidance and direction. Work is such a fundamental part of our day-to-day wellbeing; ensuring you are doing something you truly enjoy and flourish at is one of the best investments you can make in your career. I would also recommend it to any HR professionals or executive coaches to aid your work in supporting career management. This edition is packed with helpful exercises and wise advice. John's approach is a very practical and pragmatic one, helping you unlock your potential and adopt changes that will help you in a complex and often challenging employment market – throughout the various stages of your career.'
Gordon McFarland, Global Head of HR and Executive Coach, international law firm

'John brings a clarity and practical focus to helping people engage with their own career development. His choice of language and activities makes the text accessible and motivating. It really is a go-to resource for anyone who wants to invest in their own career or looking to secure a new role.'
Rosemary McLean, Director, The Career Innovation Company

'John Lees' latest edition of *How to Get a Job You Love* does not disappoint and is packed full of practical and effective strategies to land that job. There is excellent new material on, amongst other things, networking, social media and telling your story. John Lees is a recognised authority on job hunting, and I can recommend this outstanding new edition to anyone wanting to boost their chances of getting a job, or for professionals assisting others in this important task.'

Dr Jim Bright, Organisational Psychologist; Director of Research and Impact, Become Education; author of *How to write a Brilliant CV*

'I frequently recommend job seekers or those at a career crossroads to read *How to Get a Job You Love* as it offers practical and easily accessible advice from someone with vast experience in the area.'

Joëlle Warren MBE, DL, Executive Chair and Founding Partner, Warren Partners

'This book is an indispensable guide to the modern world of work and careers.'

Rhymer Rigby, journalist and author of *28 Business Thinkers Who Changed The World*

How to Get a Job You Love

Pearson

At Pearson, we have a simple mission: to help people make more of their lives through learning.

We combine innovative learning technology with trusted content and educational expertise to provide engaging and effective learning experiences that serve people wherever and whenever they are learning.

From classroom to boardroom, our curriculum materials, digital learning tools and testing programmes help to educate millions of people worldwide – more than any other private enterprise.

Every day our work helps learning flourish, and wherever learning flourishes, so do people.

To learn more, please visit us at **www.pearson.com**

How to Get a Job You Love

Find a job worth
getting up for

John Lees

Pearson

Harlow, England • London • New York • Boston • San Francisco • Toronto • Sydney
Dubai • Singapore • Hong Kong • Tokyo • Seoul • Taipei • New Delhi
Cape Town • São Paulo • Mexico City • Madrid • Amsterdam • Munich • Paris • Milan

PEARSON EDUCATION LIMITED
KAO Two
KAO Park
Harlow CM17 9NA
United Kingdom
Tel: +44 (0)1279 623623
Web: www.pearson.com

First edition published 2023 (print and electronic)
Previous editions published by McGraw Hill

ISBN: 978-1-292-46330-8 (print)
          978-1-292-73144-5 (ePub)

British Library Cataloguing-in-Publication Data
A catalogue record for the print edition is available from the British Library

Library of Congress Cataloging-in-Publication Data
A catalog record for the print edition is available from the Library of Congress

10 9 8 7 6 5 4 3 2 1
27 26 25 24 23

Cover design by Rob Watts
Cover image © KVASVECTOR/Shutterstock

Print edition typeset in 10/14 Charter ITC Pro by Straive
Printed by Ashford Colour Press Ltd, Gosport

NOTE THAT ANY PAGE CROSS REFERENCES REFER TO THE PRINT EDITION

This book, like all previous editions,
is dedicated to someone
who has been special to me
for a very long time.

To my wife, Jan
– for giving me space to find out.

Contents

**Online chapters
(go to http://go.pearson.com/uk/business)**

List of exercises

Pearson's Commitment to Diversity, Equity and Inclusion

Pearson is dedicated to creating bias-free content that reflects the diversity, depth and breadth of all learners' lived experiences. We embrace the many dimensions of diversity including, but not limited to, race, ethnicity, gender, sex, sexual orientation, socioeconomic status, ability, age and religious or political beliefs.

Education is a powerful force for equity and change in our world. It has the potential to deliver opportunities that improve lives and enable economic mobility. As we work with authors to create content for every product and service, we acknowledge our responsibility to demonstrate inclusivity and incorporate diverse scholarship so that everyone can achieve their potential through learning. As the world's leading learning company, we have a duty to help drive change and live up to our purpose to help more people create a better life for themselves and to create a better world.

Our ambition is to purposefully contribute to a world where:

- Everyone has an equitable and lifelong opportunity to succeed through learning.
- Our educational products and services are inclusive and represent the rich diversity of learners.
- Our educational content accurately reflects the histories and lived experiences of the learners we serve.
- Our educational content prompts deeper discussions with students and motivates them to expand their own learning and worldview.

We are also committed to providing products that are fully accessible to all learners. As per Pearson's guidelines for accessible educational Web media, we test and retest the capabilities of our products against the highest standards for every release, following the WCAG guidelines in developing new products for copyright year 2022 and beyond. You can learn more about Pearson's commitment to accessibility at:

https://www.pearson.com/us/accessibility.html

➤

About the author

John Lees is one of UK's best-known career strategists and the author of 15 books on work and careers. *How to Get a Job You Love* regularly features as one of the best-known career change handbooks by a British author. It was twice selected as the WHSmith Business Book of the Month and was the winner of the Australian Career Book award. John's books have been translated into Arabic, Georgian, Polish, Japanese and Spanish.

John has written career columns for *Metro* and *People Management* and wrote the introduction to the *Harvard Business Review Guide to Getting the Right Job*. He appears frequently in the national press and his work has been profiled in *Management Today, Psychologies, Coaching at Work* and *The Sunday Times*. TV appearances include *Back to Work* (BBC Interactive), *Working Lunch* (BBC2), *Dispatches* (Channel 4), *Talking Business* (BBC World), and *Tonight – How to Get a Job* (ITV). He has delivered career workshops in Australia, Germany, Ireland, New Zealand, Mauritius, Spain, South Africa, Switzerland and several parts of the USA.

John is a graduate of the universities of Cambridge, London and Liverpool, and has spent his career focusing on the world of work, spending 25 years training recruitment specialists. He is the former Chief Executive of the Institute of Employment Consultants (now the REC) and an Honorary Fellow of the REC. He served as Joint Chair of the Association of Career Professionals, UK (2011–2013), and as a founding Board Director of the Career Development Institute. He is a NICEC Fellow.

He has consulted or led workshops for a wide range of organisations including abrdn, AMBA, Boston Consulting Group, The British Council, Careershifters, Career Counselling Services, Career Development Institute, Fitzwilliam College Cambridge, Gumtree, Deutsche Bank, Hiscox, The House of Commons, ICAEW, The Institute of Leadership & Management, Imperial College, Intuit, The Association of MBAs, Lee Hecht Harrison, Lloyds Banking Group, Manpower, The Met Office, The National Audit Office, NICEC, The Officers' Association, Now Teach, Standard Life, Totaljobs, plus a wide range of business schools.

Alongside his day job, John serves as an Anglican priest in the Diocese of Exeter. He is a Prebendary of Exeter Cathedral and National Officer for Self-Supporting Ordained Ministry. He is married to the poet and painter, Jan Dean.

Career coaching support

John Lees Associates specialises in helping people make difficult career decisions – difficult either because they don't know what to do next or because there are barriers in the way. Find out more at **www.johnleescareers.com**

Career coach training

John Lees is part of the team at Firework Coaching, which provides high-impact, ICF-accredited career coach training. This training is designed to give existing coaches the confidence and credibility to work successfully with people going through career change. It does this through providing a proven framework and set of tools, including many from this book, together with a supportive community of licensed coaches around the world. Find out more at **www.fireworkcoaching.com**

Author's acknowledgements

―――――

With age comes, later than it should, a realisation of those many people I haven't thanked enough.

My gratitude goes to several special people: To Becky Charman for managing my PR brilliantly for many years. I thank Shiobhaun Watt, Senior Consultant at John Lees Associates, for her advice and encouragement and my agent James Wills at Watson, Little for his unstinting support.

I'm aware how many people have worked on this book. I thank Elizabeth Choules for commissioning the first edition, and Jane Bartlett, Andrew Lees and Stuart Mitchell for advice on shaping it. My very big thanks go to Eloise Cook at Pearson for editing this edition.

My appreciation goes out to all those who have inspired, encouraged, asked great questions and given me opportunities to road-test material: Mel Barclay, Jane Bartlett, Michelle Bayley, Will Beale, Gill Best, Jo Bond, Marie Brett, Jim Bright, Sab Byrne, Janice Chalmers, Julian Childs, Steve Crabb, James Curran, Hilary Dawson, Sara Dewar, Paul Drew, Matthias Feist, Peter Fennah, David Fouracre, Helen Green, Alison Hall, Kate Howlett, Sarah Hudson, Tudor Humphreys, Ajaz Hussain, Kathryn Jackson, Sarah

Jackson, Lisa Jones, Esi Kpeglo, Anna Levy, Susannah McClymont, Gordon McFarland, Rosemary McLean, Adi Mechen, David Morgan, Rob Nathan, Wendy Pearson, Daniel Porot, Paru Radia, Robert Rees, Rhymer Rigby, Stuart Robertson, Jackie Robinson, Valerie Rowles, Rachel Schofield, Philip Sourbut, Natasha Stanley, Louisa Taylor, Paul Thurston, Alex Volcansek, Helen Walker, Mike Williams, Ruth Winden, Julia Yates and Marie Zimenoff. I thank Gill Frigerio, Anne Futcher, David Herbert and Magdalen Smith for their thoughts on vocation. Big thanks also to Lawrence Arnold and the judging panel of the Australian Career Book award.

I thank clients who have kindly agreed to be case studies (some preserving anonymity), and a special thank you goes to Joëlle Warren and Richard Alderson for being guest contributors. A second thank you is due to Richard for letting me test ideas in the Careershifters Launch Pad and teach some of these exercises on Firework Coaching programmes.

I take this moment to remember two colleagues no longer with us who made such a difference to my writing. My friend and publicist Sue Blake made the first 10 years of being published so much fun. I also thank and acknowledge Richard Nelson Bolles, author of *What Color Is Your Parachute?* and inspirational teacher of two unforgettable summer workshops in Bend, Oregon.

Publisher's acknowledgements

Text credits:

1 Houghton Mifflin Harcourt: Lawrence, D. H. (1928) 'Work', reprinted in The Complete Poems of D.H. Lawrence. London: Heinemann (1972), p. 450; 4 THE FINANCIAL TIMES LTD: O'Connor, S. (2015) I quit! Job resignations and the UK labour puzzle, The Financial Times, 25 March, 2015. Available online: https://www.ft.com/content/632649cf-fffe-3926-bde0-9e4497d7e01d (accessed 18 April, 2023); 10 The Mental Health Foundation: Mental Health Foundation (2021) Work–Life Balance. Available online: https://www.mentalhealth.org.uk/a-to-z/w/work-lifebalance (accessed 24 April, 2023); 10 The New Press: Terkel, S. (1974) Working: People Talk About What They Do All Day and How They Feel About What They Do. New York: The New Press, p. xi; 10 Chartered Institute of Personnel and Development: CIPD. (2019) UK working lives: The CIPD job quality index. Available online: www.cipd.co.uk/Images/uk-working-livessummary-2019-v1_tcm18-58584.pdf (accessed 29 January, 2020); 10 HarperCollins: Fox, M. (1994) The Reinvention of Work. San Francisco, CA: Harper Collins, p. 33; 13 John Ruskin: Ruskin, J. (1851) Pre-Raphaelitism.

New York: John Wiley, p. 7; 25 Wordsworth Editions Ltd: Jerome, J. K. (1889) Three Men in a Boat. Ware: Wordsworth Classics (1993), p. 117; 36-38 Richard Alderson: Richard Alderson; 38 Careershifters: Careershifters; 39 Penguin Random House LLC: Kipling, R. (1910) 'If', Rewards and Fairies. New York: Doubleday, Page & Company, p. 175; 40 Penguin Random House LLC: Ferguson, M. (1987) The Aquarian Conspiracy: Personal and Social Transformation in the 1980s. New York: J.P. Tarcher, p. 112; 48 Crossroad Publishing Company: Rohr, R. (1999) Everything Belongs. New York: The Crossroad Publishing Co., p. 19; 50-51 Tariq: Tariq; 53 Holtzbrinck Publishing Holdings LP: Frost, R. (1914a) 'The death of the hired man', North of Boston. New York: Henry Holt & Co., p. 14; 65 Kathryn Jackson: Kathryn Jackson; 67 Fields, Osgood, & Company: Reade, C. (1870) Put Yourself in His Place. Boston, MA: Fields, Osgood & Co., p. 21; 71 JOSHBERSIN: Bershin, J. (2019) Let's stop talking about soft skills: They're PowerSkills. https://joshbersin.com/2019/10/lets-stop-talkingabout-soft-skills-theyre-power-skills/; 83 Roberts Brothers: Dickinson, E. (1863) Poems of Emily Dickinson. Boston, MA: Roberts Brothers, 'Poem 670', p. 203; 93 Penguin Random House LLC: Wilde, O. (1893) Lady Windermere's Fan, a Play About a Good Woman. London: Samuel French, Act 1; 107 Gilbert Keith Chesterton : Chesterton, G. K. (1905) Heretics. London: John Lane, p. 16; 121 Melissa: Melissa; 123 Holtzbrinck Publishing Holdings LP: Frost, R. (1914b) 'The self-seeker', North of Boston. New York: Henry Holt & Co, p. 61; 133 Cowley Publications: Williams, R. (1995) A Ray of Darkness: Sermons and Reflections. Lanham, MD: Cowley Publications, p. 152; 133 SPCK Publishing: Smith, M. (2019) The Grace-Filled Wilderness. London: SPCK, p. 76; 135-136 Will Beale: Will Beale; 137 Phillips, Sampson & Company: Emerson, R. W. (1840) Essays: First Series. Boston, MA: Phillips, Sampson & Company, p. 53; 153 Hachette Book Group USA: Herrick, R. (1648) 'Seeke and find', Hesperides, or the Works Both Humane and Divine of Robert Herrick Esq, Vol. 2. Boston, MA: Little, Brown & Company (1856), p. 159; 165-167 Joëlle Warren: Joëlle Warren; 169 Macmillan: Whitehead, A. N. (1925) Science and the Modern World. New York:

Macmillan, p. 4; 171 The Washington Post: Krucoff, C. (1984) The 6 o'clock scholar: Librarian of Congress Daniel Boorstin and his love affair with books. The Washington Post, 29 January, 1984, p. K8; 185 Holtzbrinck Publishing Holdings LP: James, W. (1890) The Principles of Psychology. New York: Henry Holt & Co., p. 333; 199 Wordsworth Editions Ltd: Dickens, C. (1860) Great Expectations. Ware: Wordsworth Editions (1992), p. 285; 215 The New York Times: Twain, M. (1905) A humorist's confession, The New York Times, 26 November, 1905; 218 Mary Wilson: Mary Wilson.

Image credits:

John Lees – **xiv**: John Lees; **80**: John Lees; **176**: John Lees; **176**: John Lees; **177**: John Lees; **177**: John Lees; **178**: John Lees.

Foreword

———

Whether you are a job seeker as a result of redundancy or have decided it is simply time to make a change, finding your dream role is often seen to be the Holy Grail of career management.

Working with over 20,000 individuals each year, at LHH we specialise in not only supporting people to find their next role, but also focusing on finding a job that inspires and motivates them. Considering the current economic climate and shifting market forces, we often find that our candidates feel that they can't afford the luxury of time spent seeking the ideal role and will often resort to the first job that comes along.

Interestingly, with the current demand for talent outstripping supply, job changers have enjoyed the ability to pursue dream roles, changes of sector and career re-invention in a way that has not been seen in recent years. Organisations are keen to retain their talent and are employing techniques to re-train and upskill their employees rather than lose them. However, even in this climate of career opportunities, how do individuals ensure that they are pursuing a role that will excite, fulfil and motivate them?

We know from our experience that preparing for any new role is the key to success. Those with well planned and executed strategies will succeed and are more likely to target roles that meet their values, experience and skills. Working with trained, experienced and empathetic coaches will significantly improve self-awareness and the ability to identify what you need from your next role.

A realistic assessment of core values and drivers will help you identify what really are the non-negotiables and what are the 'wish list' items on your dream job description. All this will help you make an educated and informed decision about whether the job you are looking for is the right one for you.

Fortunately, *How to Get a Job You Love* is the perfect guide to taking these steps towards managing your next career move. As with all John's career guidance, you will find pragmatic, sensible and thoughtful ideas on conducting a realistic job search which focuses on taking control of your career through effective techniques and strategies. Follow this advice and you will be on the right track to find your Holy Grail.

Mel Barclay, Head of Career Transition and Mobility,
UK and Ireland, Lee Hecht Harrison

How to use this book

———

Who is this book for?

This book is for anyone trying to make informed decisions about career choice. It will provide support and ideas if you are

- wondering how to think about career choice in a fast-changing world;
- facing redundancy, and asking, 'What do I do next?';
- feeling 'stuck' and looking for new challenges, and wondering, 'What on earth can I do?';
- deciding how to reinvent yourself mid-career;
- unemployed and looking for quicker ways of identifying interesting opportunities;
- seeking work and hitting a brick wall with applications;
- discouraged because you believe you have little to offer the labour market;
- attracted by the idea of changing career but don't know how to begin.

How this book might help you

This book is written to provide shortcuts for anyone job hunting, and especially for someone interested in career change – the kind of person who says the statement I hear so often: 'I know I want to do something different, but I don't know what it is.'

This is a book about career change. That might mean doing something better, and might mean something different. The book's title isn't misleading. You *can* get a job you love – certainly one you love more than anything else you've done before. A job that feels like a better life deal. To do so, you'll need to do some imagining, some reflecting and a lot of doing – including things you've never done before.

You might already have looked at books that tell you how to job hunt or write a CV – books that work if you know what you want and you just need a strategy to get it. This book takes a different approach. My belief is that the biggest, most ambitious career breakthroughs happen because people do two things differently.

First, they learn to think – in new ways, reframing, getting a new perspective, examining the self-defeating language that gets in our way. We all want to feel encouraged, aware of strengths, and able to talk about them authentically – that's the direction of travel in these chapters.

Second, people learn how to put ideas into action, taking the first step towards something new. This doesn't mean applying for the first job you see, but learning how to be more experimental, how to carry on when you feel dispirited and avoiding some of the more obvious minefields along the way.

I've drawn on decades of experience to write this book – thousands of coaching sessions and conversations with everyone from community job clubs to executive career changers, and ideas fine-tuned in workshops and webinars. I've refined the tools by teaching them to fellow career coaches. Before working as a career coach, I spent many years training recruitment consultants to be better interviewers. I've included every shortcut I can think of, especially techniques for reaching people, getting shortlisted and shining at interviews.

What underpins this book is the idea I played with when writing the first edition: 'What happens if we apply business creativity to the way people change careers?' Organisations reinvent themselves every day, rebranding, diversifying, moving into new sectors. How can you and I apply some of that creative thinking to career choice?

Read on and you will find tools for incremental change, and strategies for making a bigger transformation. You may discover that you don't need to jump ship in order to improve your work – understanding what makes work more stimulating may lead to exploring new possibilities in your current role or organisation.

This book aims to unlock your hidden potential and make your waking hours more creative, more meaningful, more enjoyable. It will show you new ways of exploring. It will encourage you to propel yourself towards a job that feels worth getting up for on a cold Monday morning.

How to use this book

How to Get a Job You Love is designed to be a complete career change programme in one volume. You may read it in a couple of days, or even in a few hours. It offers tips, ways forward and exercises to prompt reflection. It might give you something you need right now, but I hope it feels like an unfolding conversation, supporting you as you think, learn and try things out.

If you find yourself thinking, 'I don't have time for all this', think again. You are considering your career, not choosing your next smartphone or a holiday destination. Work absorbs a big chunk of your life. The decisions prompted by this book can easily impact your work for decades ahead. So, make time – invest time in your future.

Don't feel compelled to read this book front to back like a novel. Jump to sections which look interesting, exercises that speak to you, or tips you need most urgently. You may find that a single exercise unlocks something important, or you build up a picture using several exercises (bring key information together in the **ideas grid** on p. 217). If an exercise or idea doesn't work for you, don't feel you've 'failed'. All it means is this: *the exercise doesn't work for you.* Put it aside and move on.

The initial chapters focus on the way we think about work, and psychological barriers to change. The middle section of the book offers you a toolkit for self-discovery, exploring your career hot buttons, your hidden and motivated skills, your chosen areas of knowledge and the key aspects of personality that will shape your career. You'll also find material on choosing a career that feels worth doing, practical advice on choosing work sectors and key material on career change. Everything else is about making connections, searching and job hunting more effectively (including online strategies), conducting information interviews and doing brilliantly at interview.

Chapter 3 gives you the opportunity to take a useful free online **Career change test** from Careershifters (see p. 38).

Under time pressure? Chapter 14 offers a 4-hour job search programme showing you how to make best use of your time and achieve quick results.

At the end of most chapters you'll find a short **case study** based on someone who has benefited from ideas in this book.

New in this edition

If you're familiar with the earlier editions, you will notice many changes and revisions, plus these new features:

- A new Chapter 11 ('Dealing with knockbacks, and getting stuck')
- New material on online interviews and selection processes
- Updated material on online job hunting and using social media
- Exercise 6.3 – Skill movie trailer

- Exercise 11.1 – Getting unstuck
- Chapter 13 – Springboard conversations (a new format for information interviews)
- Exercise 14.2 – Rewind the video
- Exercise 16.1 – Ideas grid.

Downloadable exercises and chapters

See p. ix for a list of all the exercises in this book. You will notice that there are three additional online chapters. All exercises and chapters can be downloaded free of charge from http://go.pearson.com/uk/business.

James, games industry professional

James had a senior leadership position in publishing. Although he never took the role for granted, he wondered if he might have found a job for life. However, following an organisational restructure he left the company.

'My life was turned upside down', he explains. 'I went from what I thought was a stable and secure job to having no idea what I wanted to do next.'

How to Get a Job You Love helped James understand what motivated him professionally and how transferable skills would find him a new role. 'My biggest problem was a lack of confidence', James remembers. 'I was unfamiliar with the market. I built up limiting beliefs in my head. This work helped me challenge assumptions and think about how to access the hidden job market.'

Through his network, James learned of a strategic marketing role in the games industry, in a company he'd always been keen to work for. 'As it turned out, the company had been struggling

➤

---

to find the right person. I didn't have an obvious background but knew how to translate my skills.'

'Looking back, after a decade in book publishing, I wouldn't have believed such a move was possible. By letting go of preconceptions, I was able to grow both personally and professionally, and turn the corner during a very tough period of my life.'

chapter 1

'Get a job I love?' Get real . . .

'There is no point in work unless it absorbs you like an absorbing game.'

D.H. Lawrence (1928)

> This chapter helps you to
> - think more deeply about work satisfaction;
> - gain insights into a rapidly changing job market;
> - learn how job hunting has altered dramatically;
> - understand how to start to take control of your career;
> - move out of passive, 'default' mode.

Why should people be happy at work ?

I have found myself in a bookshop standing next to someone picking up this book. If they're with a friend, they sometimes read the title out loud to get a reaction. I'm always interested to hear the reply. It will be anything from 'sounds interesting' to a cynical 'hmmm . . . *I wish*'.

It's easy to believe that having a job you love is a fantasy. Work isn't about enjoying yourself, surely? It's not supposed to be fun, your friends will tell you. Work is about hard-nosed reality. If that sounds like a universal truth, look again at people who seem to get something different out of their working lives. You spot them because they talk about work with energy. They're making new things happen, sharing what they know, inspiring people, making a difference in society. Some produce brilliant ideas, products or great experiences for customers. Some work for themselves, others work for organisations they believe in. They have a job they love doing most days of the week. Are they richer or poorer as a result? Happiness and success don't always come hand in hand, but be clear: *being unhappy is no automatic route to success*. Unhappy, disengaged people are often the ones companies get rid of first.

There is a kind of strange career pact we seem to make. This pact assumes, 'I can only be successful if . . . '. Here are some examples: 'I can only be a top salesperson if I work long hours and eat badly'; 'I can only be a great manager if I don't empathise with my staff.' Listen to the language people use when they decide to compromise. They 'settle for' choices they're not really comfortable with. They 'lower their sights'. They pretend they are being logical.

The days of your life

Why should people be happy at work? Take a deep breath. Read that question again. Work is where you might spend most of your waking life for four decades, or more.

According to UK government statistics, females born this decade have an average lifespan of around 84 years. Call it 31,000 days. Men get less – about 29,000 days. So, maybe 30,000 days to learn, work, play, raise a family, leave your mark on life and acquire wisdom. If you live to 50, statistically you'll get longer than this, but even so, 30,000 days doesn't sound like a lot of time, does it? Especially if you're saying, 'This isn't what I wanted to do when I grew up . . . '.

If you work full-time hours, you spend more time at work than at any other waking activity. If you live for 70 years, you'll spend about 23 of those years asleep and 16 years working. You will spend over 100,000 hours of your life working, and the 24/7 economy demands more and more. Work is where you put about 80 per cent of your best attention. How much time do you spend planning for work, worrying about work, complaining about work? Yes, you do things outside work, but work requires a huge chunk of your stamina, imagination and personal energy. Work matters. It contributes to self-esteem, personal fulfilment, learning and relationships. Choosing how you spend Monday to Friday is one of the most important life decisions you will ever make.

So the question, 'Why should people be happy at work?' really means *why should people be happy?* What do you think? Do happy people live longer, stay healthier, have great children and make a difference? You know they do. So let's stop that Faustian deal: 'I can only get a great job if I forget about being happy at work.' That's a self fulfilling deal. Be careful what you ask for – you might just get it.

Work in a changing world

Publishing a book called *How to Get a Job You Love* has required nerve in a rapidly changing society. In early 2020 we were still recovering from the turbulence of the 'great recession' when the pandemic hit, resulting in many huge changes, including a rise in hybrid home and office working. This international homeworking experiment will probably change work forever. We have seen skill shortages, older workers leaving the labour market early and a cost of living crisis. War in Ukraine, energy prices, political turmoil . . . the impact of these multiple layers of disruption unfold daily.

Some future trends are clear. Unprecedented recent funding into healthcare, pharmaceuticals and IT offer huge possibilities. Technology will continue to become faster and cheaper, enhanced by artificial intelligence. ChatGPT and its successors will transform content creation. Today's video meeting platforms will seem antiquated and unresponsive in a few years, replaced by software which more authentically replicates real conversations.

Workers continue to express concern about long working hours, pay, worrying that their job might change or disappear. Others face the challenges of insecure and low paid work, zero hours contracts and working poverty. Those over 50 face challenges, but not as great as those faced by 16–24 year olds. Many experience repeated cycles of uncertainty, change, restructuring and redundancy. If job change is forced on some workers, for some it's an attractive option. FT journalist Sarah O'Connor (2015) looks at the numbers who choose to resign from a job in order to take up another, calling it the 'Take This Job and Shove It Index'.

One feature of modern life is the challenge of predicting even the short-term future. Jobs seem hard to fill, but at the same time employers are so cautious they build in extra selection stages, or rethink jobs halfway through a hiring process. Candidates increasingly complain about being 'ghosted', summarily dropped without explanation or feedback – doing nothing for confidence.

Where organisations have restructured extensively, the psychological contract has been weakened, if not torn up. This is most obvious where staff have to apply for their own jobs, or have to perform work previously done by two workers. A research study (de Jong et al. 2016) revealed that when organisations restructure, there is a measurably negative effect on employee well-being – even when there are no job losses. This has inevitable implications for engagement and loyalty.

We all know people affected by redundancy. During and after lockdown, business closures and layoffs have been commonplace. This has one positive aspect: Employers see so many candidates who have been 'let go', they don't ask why.

What career path?

Organisations continue to become leaner, chasing efficiency savings. As a result, they have become flatter: tiers of management have been removed, and workers are expected to cover a wider range of tasks. The lack of obvious pathways for promotion can be disorienting – individuals have to make lateral moves to advance. Such moves often require highly developed relationship-building and networking skills.

There was a time when most organisations offered career futures – promotion ladders, development opportunities to assure workers that they would be retained and valued. These structures are hard to find in today's market. Employers are becoming more transparent about what they can really offer – something closer to a work *project*. This will still be a valuable block of experience, but with an expiry date. Soon, the idea of long-term talent retention may seem like an antiquated, old-century idea. The gig economy doesn't just apply to freelancers – many Gen Z workers acknowledge weak ties to organisations and a plan for job mobility and experiment.

Career decision making has become more complex, especially the classic question, 'Do I go or do I stay?' Some change roles because of a lack of a pay raise or promotion, but with an unclear sense of what they're moving into. Those who stay may wait for a tap on the shoulder that never comes. Many find themselves looking for a new role without really knowing what they want. There's also a growing trend of heightened awareness of career satisfaction, often expressed as a search for purpose or meaning. Others take a pragmatic approach: 'If I'm going to lose my job, I might as well find something interesting.'

Something interesting has happened in the world of work. Looking back over the years, job hunting has changed dramatically. Until the early part of this century, jobs were much more visible. Many of them were advertised, involving a straightforward application process. Since then, many have gone under the radar – a much smaller proportion are advertised conventionally. Employers have learned many cheap and smart ways of attracting talent. Sometimes this is high-tech (for example, attracting crowds of would-be workers to websites). Others use a canny mix of social media, organisational job boards and word of mouth.

In today's marketplace, jobs are increasingly filled by low-cost, low-visibility, informal methods. This is the 'hidden' job market (see Chapter 12). Looking for a job effectively means spending less time on internet searching and form filling, and more on conversations and connections. If this seems daunting, don't despair. This book outlines a wide range of shortcuts.

Taking control for the first time

When the rules of the game change every year, we all need more control over our careers. Many people are passive about career decisions. They talk about being flattered or pushed into jobs, and they talk about where they have 'ended up'. They make choices based on an out-of-date picture of work. Many choose to cruise on autopilot, seeing what comes along.

Passive thinking allows life to go on around us. It's easy to shrug off responsibility with a phrase like 'A job's a job. It pays the bills. Jobs are hard to find.' New occupations are opening up all the time, and during a working lifetime we are sampling a bigger range of them. Pension insecurity means working longer, but this can increase opportunities for career refreshment.

When you're trying to reposition yourself in the job market, two things really help: optimism and curiosity. Optimistic thinking keeps the end in mind, encouraging you to keep pushing on doors, asking questions. Curiosity compels you to do so. Exploration is the key activity in career change because there's more out there than you know. In a typical year, one in ten people change jobs – that's in addition to people entering work for the first time. Also, new *types* of jobs are invented all the time.

If you want a new job, the market isn't straightforward. If you want to change careers, things can seem very slippery. You'll need resilience to cope with the roller-coaster ride of job hunting. Conventional job searching (see Chapter 12) means you will hear a lot of silence – the most commonly experienced market reaction. Chasing advertised positions can mean a lot of effort with zero return. Many employers freely acknowledge that they don't respond to job applications unless they are inviting candidates to interview.

Reframing helps. How often do you hear criticism and clutch it to yourself as the last, final and totally accurate picture of *you*? Human beings find it easy to ignore positive information, and distort neutral information into something negative. Watch out for limitations you put in your own way – favourite internal scripts like 'it's all about who you know. . .'.

Some people find interesting and well-paid work even when opportunities are thin on the ground. Are they lucky? Sometimes. The rest is down to how they choose to think, and how they choose to *act*. Examine the way you think about opportunity, luck and change. Do you see closed doors, or doors with handles? *Ah, that depends. . .* and it does. It depends *how you look*. Look for possibilities, not barriers.

Many job hunters believe that looking for jobs is as straightforward as opening a new account with an online retailer – a simple matter of entering data onto screens. The reality is different. Today, looking for a new role (particularly a senior job, a creative job or a job in a niche or new sector) requires sophisticated skills in influencing, communicating, savvy use of social media and the ability to build relationships quickly. The process is less like form filling and more like *trying to get elected to public office*. You need to influence key decision makers, followers, ambassadors and champions. Most of all, you need to learn how to be visible – so *jobs find you*.

Exercise 1.1
Breaking out of default mode

- -

Electronic devices have a 'default mode', often the original factory settings. When you're looking for a new job, employers, recruiters and other contacts make assumptions about what you're looking for. For example, recruitment agencies may assume you want a similar role to the one you held most recently.

Think about the 'default mode' your career suggests, using the prompts below.

	What role will people expect you to undertake next in 'default mode' . . .
Based on your last job?	
Based on your career history?	
Based on page 1 of your CV?	
Based on your LinkedIn profile?	
Based on your most recent qualifications or training?	

What would you really like to do? What would you call that job?

If you can't name the job, how is it different from the 'default' jobs listed above?

What you get out of work, and what work gets out of you

The word 'career' comes from the Latin *carrus*, a wheeled vehicle (linked to 'chariot' or 'carriage'). In other words, it's a vehicle that takes us through life. Another use of the word is to move in an uncontrolled direction, as in, 'The steering failed, and my car careered across the motorway'. Random movement in an uncontrolled direction. Does that sound familiar?

A lot of research has been undertaken in the last two decades on worker engagement. Only a small proportion of employees feel committed to their work, and many are likely to leave the job if another opportunity presents itself. Surveys reveal that work satisfaction has declined in the past 30 years with the main factor being lengthening working hours. The Mental Health Foundation (2021) found that 'The cumulative effect of increased working hours is having an important effect on the lifestyle of a huge number of people, which is likely to prove damaging to their mental well-being'. US writer Studs Terkel (1974) famously recorded that work, for some, was 'A Monday to Friday sort of dying'.

On the other hand, engaged workers often say they would continue in the same job if they had a multimillion lottery win. Motivation is a complicated arena. My grandfather Owen Roberts had a way with words in both Welsh and English. He said, 'I eat well, I sleep well, and when I think about work I tremble all over'. It wasn't true, of course. He spent many contented years working as a dockside blacksmith.

Is work that important? Judging by the amount of time spent complaining about work, it must be. If it wasn't for work, we would have far less to moan about. We put a huge amount of our lives into work and rely on it for a large slice of self-esteem. For this reason alone, unemployment and underemployment are damaging. Equally, people who don't find their work engaging can feel that life lacks something.

Work can provide excitement, variety, friendship, challenge and continuous learning. Even so, it's easy for work to play too big a part in your identity. Your family may rely on your pay packet, but they may bear some of the cost of your commitment to work. A CIPD Survey (2019) placed the UK 24th out of 25 economies in terms of quality of work–life balance. The survey indicates that 'Overwork is most common among managerial and professional workers. It is also more common among those who work from home, showing that flexible working may not always solve tensions between work and personal life and may even contribute to the blurring of the boundaries between them.' Matthew Fox (1994) wrote, 'Behind some parental compulsion to bring home exaggerated amounts of pay is often a flight from the joy of living life here and now in the family – as if the future were more important than the present . . . We ought not to postpone living because of work or because of our plans for buying something with the money we make.'

In the 1970s, an old joke was popularised by the comedian Lily Tomlin: *Even if you win the rat race, you're still a rat.* You might want to find a job you love. You might also need a strategy to find a job that builds you up more than it breaks you down.

Simon, insurance analyst and former TV location scout

Simon felt that he had reached an important crossroads in his career. He'd worked in numerous sectors including construction, health and safety, event management and property finance, and decided to investigate other options including areas that he hadn't taken the opportunity to explore in the past.

He discovered that his interest in buildings and property could be transferred to the TV and film industry, particularly finding locations for filming. Simon explains: 'The TV industry can be perceived as a closed shop that can't be entered unless you are in the know, but if you are determined enough, you can find a way in.' A chance conversation opened a door, and Simon started to make contact with various location managers.

The process was challenging: 'I gathered a list of people working in the area and contacted everybody in turn, with the initial purpose of asking them about their work, and any tips they could offer going forward, using information interviews.' Simon persevered in building relationships, and after four months he got his first job as a location assistant on a production for the BBC, enjoying the industry for a couple of years before consciously moving back to an enjoyable role in financial services.

chapter 2

Overcoming barriers to change

'No small misery is caused by overworked and unhappy people, in the dark views which they necessarily take up themselves, and force upon others, of work itself.'

John Ruskin (1851)

This chapter helps you to

- understand your confidence window;
- identify the blocks between you and a great career;
- name and shame barriers to progress;
- define your preferred time balance in a job.

Your confidence window

When you're looking for a new role or considering career change, time matters. Researching opportunities and persuading people to talk to you takes time. Time is important for another reason – confidence.

At the beginning of a job hunt, people are generally optimistic, happy to take new ideas on board. As you experience the reality of the job market, this confidence can fade. You might experience a confidence 'window'.

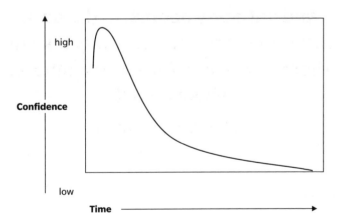

Early on, even if you've just lost a job, you might feel the elation of the new – everything's to play for. Feeling positive, you throw yourself at jobs you don't understand, probably with an unconvincing CV. The results you get quickly dampen confidence. When you hear nothing at all, you suspect the worst about your offer. Soon you start tinkering with your CV – without knowing what to change.

Other results slow you down. You contact a recruitment agency who say they can't place you. Friends and family tell you to 'take what you can get'. You start to feel that you don't have what employers want. You network a little, but ineffectively, and decide it's a waste of time. Your interview performance starts to go off the boil. You're tempted to apply for any role you see.

Exercise 2.1
Constraints

We all have constraints, but each of us thinks that our constraints are uniquely limiting. Tick the constraints that apply to you.

❏ I am too old	❏ I don't have many
❏ I am underqualified	achievements
❏ My experience is all in one	❏ I worry about taking risks
industry	❏ Don't know what I want to do
❏ I have a health problem	next
❏ Location	❏ Worry that I will be out of work
❏ Travel	for a long time
❏ Lack of information about the	❏ Fear of employer's attitude to
job market	redundancy
❏ The stigma of unemployment	❏ Lack of up-to-date skills
❏ Financial commitments	❏ Fear of rejection
❏ Family/personal problems	❏ Lack of relevant qualifications
❏ Fear of approaching people	❏ Worry about having to retrain/
❏ Lack of confidence selling	go back to full-time study
myself in person	❏ I want a job that looks good on
❏ My job search to date hasn't	my CV
worked	❏ I have never had to apply for a
❏ Don't want to make the wrong	job before
decision at my time of life	❏ I don't interview well

This story might sound over-bleak, but it happens all the time. The good news is that confidence can be reinforced at every stage. If your job hunting isn't working, press 'pause'. Work out what you want to say and who you want to talk to. Use this book to spot shortcuts and ways of getting in front of interesting people. Anticipate rejection: plan to spend time with supportive friends when you experience 'no' (see Chapter 11). Next, tackle your constraints.

Look at the constraints you've ticked above. Highlight the ones which worry you most. When have you overcome them in the past? How?

Look at the constraints you have little control over – for example, travel-to-work distance or working hours if you have family responsibilities. Identifying hard constraints can be helpful because it can show you where to focus your attention. Some constraints simply describe learning needs: 'I don't interview well' means it's time for practice.

Psychological constraints are the most powerful, such as 'I don't want to make the wrong decision at my time of life'. These limit what you think is possible.

Dealing with 'yes, but. . . '

At this point, you may be hearing two familiar words in your head: 'yes, but . . . '. This is your ancient brain speaking – the part attuned to risk and safety. It's the senior committee member who attends every meeting in your brain and says, 'You tried this once and it failed', 'It'll never fly' or 'You don't have what it takes'.

'Yes, but' is closed thinking blocking any kind of change: 'Yes, but I have to earn a living', 'Yes, but in the real world . . . '. It feels like risk avoidance, but it's all about staying well inside your comfort zone. 'Yes, but' allows you to pretend that you're making a sensible decision. You'll justify it using all the old phrases: 'The grass is always greener . . . ', 'Better the devil you know . . . '.

'Yes, but' thinking gives you plenty of logical, safety-first reasons to stop before you start.

Not deciding

You might feel under pressure to decide, make a choice – prompted by questions such as 'Do I change jobs?' or 'What roles should I apply for?' Put decision making to one side because it won't help you. If you *believe* you need to make a decision, you will probably start *thinking in circles*. You know how it happens: You play with an idea, get excited by possibilities, then you meet an obstacle, so drop the idea and start circling again. These never-ending circles are poor idea building dressed up as decision making.

You don't need to make a big decision right now. In fact, it's best if you don't. Apart from one small decision: to *start somewhere*. Find out, ask questions, follow your curiosity. Just look. Take one small step of discovery – one phone call, one email, one exploratory conversation with someone who seems to be in an interesting role. The 'yes, but' mindset stops you in your tracks, ensuring that you fail before you try anything.

Personal barriers, and creative ways to leap over them

I'm frightened of making mistakes. The world's greatest inventions are the result of mistakes. Mistakes are simply feedback on our performance. Winners make far more mistakes than losers – the more they try, the more they learn. The timid mind stops after one mistake.

I don't know what I'm looking for. You might assume that you can't work on career change without knowing where you're going. The reality is you can't find a direction without drawing a map. Don't apologise for uncertainty, just say, enthusiastically, 'I'm exploring'.

Rejection feels really painful. In a job search you will probably be rejected more times than you are accepted. This is a statistical fact, not a reflection of your experience. Plan for rejection. Learn from each application, stop overprocessing and find encouragement. Abraham Lincoln carried with him a newspaper clipping stating that he was a great leader. John Lennon's school report suggested he was on the road to failure.

I don't interview well. Absolute statements like this set you up to fail. Start with small steps: catalogue what you've done and learn how to talk about it. Prepare for difficult questions (see Chapter 15).

I don't like talking about myself. Some people find it embarrassing to talk about their skills; in some cultures people dislike being seen as distinctive. Practise with supportive friends or a coach – get used to talking about your skills, work history and things you have done well – in a relaxed, authentic way.

Other people drag me down. Don't let other people live your career for you. Some people are *drains*: they react negatively to your ideas; you spend a lot of time managing their pessimism. Others are more like *radiators.* They broadcast energy, encouraging and inspiring. Radiators will say 'go for it'. Drains tell you to be 'realistic' (see Chapter 11).

Protect your ideas. New ideas need nurturing. Sometimes the worst thing you can do is to share them with the wrong kind of people and have them dismissed or trashed. Share ideas for exploration with positive-minded people.

There are no jobs out there. As Chapter 12 reveals, jobs are increasingly off-radar. Every day people leave jobs or retire and new roles are created, sometimes when employers don't seem to be hiring. What's important is this: the economy isn't in your head. Look for organisational needs, not just job vacancies.

I can't get on with it . . . Start with small goals – and stick to them. Plan your week ahead: find someone to take out for coffee so you can explore ideas and practise talking about your work history.

I'm finding job hunting exhausting. Watch your energy levels. As you begin exploring, your enthusiasm is high. It can easily flag – often when you hit the first obstacle. Plan *now* to talk to someone positive at that critical time. Get other people to make you accountable for your short-term goals.

I'm never going to be as good as other people applying. Don't make the mistake of thinking you're in competition with everyone else. You're not. You're up against the requirements of specific jobs and the needs of particular employers.

I wonder if I do really want to change. If you find yourself saying, 'My current role isn't so bad . . . I should feel lucky to have a job. . . the pay's good. . . ', look again at how closely your current role matches your motivated skills (see Chapter 6).

I'll never earn what I earn here. Ask yourself if you're really saying, 'I'm overpaid here, and no other employer will let me get away with it'. Few people stay overpaid for long. If you're making a big hole in the payroll and not delivering much in return, this is a good time to rethink.

It feels like jumping off a cliff. Fear of getting career decisions wrong can be disabling. Being motivated to *avoid* danger may mean little energy goes into exploration. Incremental thinking only gets you incremental results. Change happens when you do at least one thing differently.

There are no choices. Just get some perspective on that statement. Compared with most of the world's population, people in developed economies have a huge range of life choices, and more protection against failure. We all have choices. Some people find brilliant jobs even in the depths of a recession. Every year for the past 25 years clients have said to me, 'This is a really bad year to be changing jobs'.

I'm too old. You can find organisations that are 'young' cultures, where it can be hard for older workers to break in. If the employer wants a 19 year old to burn out in 18 months, do you want to be there anyway? Some employers realise that older workers can of course offer commitment, wisdom, common sense and reliability. Age becomes a factor if you draw attention to it. At interview don't talk about how things 'used to be done' or confess that you find modern technology or social media mystifying.

I don't have the qualifications. Formal qualifications are often less relevant than people think. Employers struggle to understand the alphabet soup of degrees and diplomas. Where a specific qualification is required, ask yourself, 'Why do they need this? What problems will it solve?' Relevant experience is often a valid alternative to paper qualifications.

I don't have the money to retrain. Don't assume that career change means full-time retraining. Research the facts. If you think you need a qualification, find out if it will improve your employability or just put a hole in your bank balance. Look for alternative routes. Is this something you can learn in your own time? Can you learn on the job?

I don't do digital. At one time using a computer was considered a specialised skill. Now toddlers do it; it's not rocket science. Get connected, and check your email at least once a day. The web makes a million things easier: research, finding people to speak to, discovering new ideas, tracking down former colleagues, seeking recommendations and endorsements. Trying to achieve this without using the internet is rather like trying to cook a three-course meal over a candle flame – an unnecessary challenge providing results very, *very* slowly.

I might be found out. It's surprising how many senior staff share a common fear: *one day I'll be found out.* This is the **impostor syndrome**, first recognised in the 1970s, and widely experienced. Many people believe they got a job through luck and they are fakes. Their secret fear is that one day their boss will say, 'Okay, we know it's been a big pretence. Just leave now and we'll say nothing more about it.' A worrying number of people would leave the building without protest. The strange thing is that most workers assume that top-level bosses are immune to this feeling. In fact, many senior staff are so isolated they spend more energy than anyone else coping with feeling like an impostor.

I can't summon up the energy to change career. If you're in work that no longer floats your boat, it's easy to feel the only solution is job change. Review your current job and look at what you might like to change. Is it the role, the people around you, the organisation or something else? What parts of the job make the time pass quickly? Ask for a career conversation. Retaining people is much cheaper than hiring new staff, and you may get better results fixing the job you are in rather than going to the market to find a new one. Use Exercise 2.2 to think about how you might use time at work more enjoyably and more productively.

I just need a job. You may by now be thinking that this advice is for other people, not you. You feel you need something that pays the bills, right now. Some years ago I worked with a group of jobseekers in a Johannesburg township. One of them, Gugu, was aged 17 and had given up looking for work. Why? 'There are no jobs in South Africa', she said. I pointed out that new jobs were being created in that country every day. 'Yes, but so many people are chasing them', she said sadly. Talking to her I realised that all over the world too many people say, 'I'll do anything', which is a great way of saying that you have nothing special to offer. Fortunately, Gugu and her fellow jobseekers all found jobs as a result of a programme encouraging them to feel confident about their abilities and experience.

No, it's true: I just need a job. Perhaps an inner voice is saying, 'Get *real* – looking for an enjoyable job is self-indulgence, a daydream.' How many excuses do you need to have to ensure you stay miserable at work? Listen to successful people talking about the work they do. They don't often say, 'Well, the money's good'. They talk about work being like a 'game', or they talk about doing work they would gladly do for nothing.

(If you discover more barriers or things that slow down discovery and change, look at Chapter 11.)

Exercise 2.2
Time balance
- -

How would you like to spend your time at work? What would be the ideal time balance?

Think about your current or most recent job. In the left-hand column, estimate the percentage of time you spend in each kind of activity. In the right-hand column, state your preferred time allocation, again as a percentage. Each column should add up to 100.

Actual %	Activity	Preferred %
	Working entirely alone Working on my own without distraction. Working things out, being given space to sort out a problem or finish a piece of work, writing something, having time to reflect . . .	
	Working independently but close to colleagues Being responsible for own results but having colleagues around. Having ready access to the ideas and encouragement of other people . . .	
	Working 1:1 Explaining, persuading, influencing, selling, coaching, managing, teaching . . .	
	Attending meetings Meeting to deal with agendas, share information and make collective decisions . . .	
	Working in active teams Group problem solving, planning, brainstorming, reviewing, getting things done, training, motivating . . .	
	Extending your network Telephoning new contacts, networking, meeting plenty of new people, going to conferences, seminars . . .	
	Working with an audience Public speaking, performing, entertaining, giving talks, informing larger groups . . .	
100%	Total	**100%**

When you have completed the time balance exercise, compare your current role with your ideal. This isn't self-indulgence or fantasy – it's a healthy recognition of how you work at your best. Look at the activities where you spend most of your time. Which would you like to increase or decrease, substantially? What difference would that make to your effectiveness?

Jan, writer and painter

Jan worked as a writer in schools, but had a strong interest in creating art. However, one big barrier discouraged her from taking any kind of art class: *I can't draw.* It seemed to be true – any attempts produced poor results.

Coaching led Jan to Betty Edwards' book *Drawing on the Right Side of the Brain* (a book sometimes used to help people in career change because of its power to help people – literally – to see things differently). Jan writes: 'The book shows you how to draw what's there, not what you think *ought* to be there. Often what you're drawing is the gaps between objects – 'negative space'. Once you switch off the part of your brain that decides what something should look like and just draw what's there, you get really different results.'

Now painting (and selling) abstract landscapes, Jan remembers the turning point: 'The problem was that I had unconsciously turned *I can't draw* into *I can't draw – ever.* I just needed to stop overthinking, do one thing differently and try a new approach. Now I love drawing – especially in charcoal. It's interesting how that word "ever" just sat there and stopped me without me noticing.'

chapter 3

First steps towards a new career deal

'I like work: it fascinates me.

I can sit and look at it for hours.'

Jerome K. Jerome (1889)

This chapter helps you to
- understand more about happiness and role satisfaction;
- think of work as a healthy, managed deal;
- capture and communicate energy;
- experiment with small steps and shift projects;
- take an online questionnaire to help with the process of career change.

Revisiting happiness

Are some occupations more likely to increase happiness? We seem to have a fascination with the worst and the best jobs in society. Popularity contests are won by surprising jobs (statisticians and web designers, for example), and more predictably by roles with positive outcomes such as childcare workers, fitness coaches and bar workers. Low job satisfaction is often recorded among teachers, social workers and health sector workers.

It's worth saying a little more about happiness. You might think that happiness is a subjective state of mind you can do little to change. Richard Layard (2005) showed that happiness can be measured objectively and contributes to good health. Exploring why some nations are happier than others, he looked at the relationship between income and happiness. He found (unsurprisingly) that if you don't have enough to live on, your happiness is reduced. When people do have enough income to cover their needs, they are generally happy. You might assume that anything earned above this level increases happiness. In fact, Layard finds that happiness doesn't increase as income rises. Being well off, even rich, doesn't make you happier. Many countries in the developing world with low income levels are more content than developed nations.

Layard also explores what aspects of work make workers discontented. One important factor isn't hard work or long hours, but *autonomy* – workers are more content where they have some control over *how* they work, when and how tasks are done as part of a reasonably predictable workload.

Think about factors which contribute to *your* long-term happiness, including mental and physical health, family relationships, friendships or belonging to a community. Work plays a big part. Being unemployed or underemployed damages self-esteem; engaging, purposeful work builds it. This is where it's useful to see your *motivated skills* (see Chapter 6) – the skills you relish using, the tasks you enjoy because they feel worth doing. Motivation turns an errand into a quest, a task into a joy.

Work satisfaction is often connected with the people you interact with. For some, it's about doing something which meets a need, solves a problem or in some other way contributes to someone else's quality of life. This is an important reminder in a rather self-focused age: one of the strongest factors affecting happiness is the opportunity to help other people.

Exercise 3.1
How happy are you in your work?

Tick the box next to the description which best describes your work right now.

❑ **Great job**

I often feel I can't wait to get into work. Work is the place where I grow and learn most, where I am set healthy challenges, where I am valued and appreciated. A great deal of fun and self-esteem is centred in my work, which fits my values, talents and personality. I know that I make a difference. I express who I am in my job. The rewards are right, and I would be happy to be paid less if necessary. I love the part work plays In my life.

❏ Thumbs up

I enjoy work most of the time, but sometimes there are headaches and problems. My work feels useful and contributes to my self-esteem. My contribution is clear, acknowledged and significant. My career is a good match to my talents, personality and values. I am appreciated by others. I feel I make a difference, and that I add something positive to the organisation. I find supervision helpful, but my boss is more a mentor than a supervisor. I lead a satisfying career which contributes to all parts of my life.

❏ Mustn't grumble

The work I do is OK. Sometimes I feel valued, other times exploited or ignored. Work is stable, largely unexciting, doesn't interfere with my inner life too much. New ways of doing things are sometimes discouraged. I may be in the right line of work, but in the wrong organisation. I am valued for some of what I do, but not always the most important things.

❏ Someone's got to do it

I work because I need to. I don't feel I owe a great deal to my employer. Several parts of the job are unpleasant/boring/demeaning/pointless. Real life begins at five o'clock. I'm not learning anything. I try to make a contribution but sometimes hit a brick wall. My skills are getting rusty. I would just like a quiet life.

❏ Clock watcher

There are days I almost have to drag myself to work; every day and every moment are miserable. I feel a huge mismatch between the person I am and the person this job requires me to be. I feel trapped. Each day makes things seem worse. I dread the prospect of Monday morning. I take all my sick leave because the job often makes me feel ill.

Exercise 3.2
If all jobs paid the same . . .

- -

Ask yourself the following question: 'If all jobs paid the same, what would I do for a living?' Having reflected on that question, fill in the four clouds below. You don't have to complete them in order.

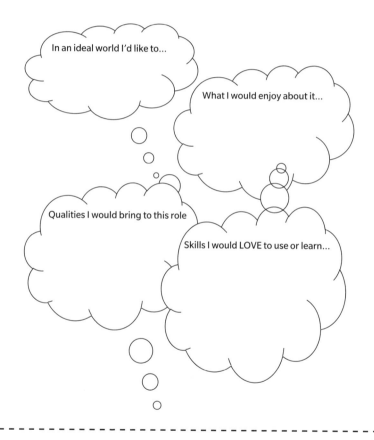

In an ideal world I'd like to...

What I would enjoy about it...

Qualities I would bring to this role

Skills I would LOVE to use or learn...

- -

Look at your answers to Exercise 3.2. How did you feel when you saw the first empty cloud? What was easy? What was difficult? For career coaches this exercise provides information about confidence, optimism, imagination, and also what gets in the way – the 'yes, buts' that are lead weights on a soul hungry for flight.

When used with groups, this exercise reveals the prevailing mindset. Some people start writing without hesitation; others find it difficult (or are reluctant) to commit thoughts to paper. One might say, 'This doesn't relate to the real world.' And that's partly what this exercise is about, to show where someone sits on the spectrum between 'ideal' and 'real'. Think of it as a seesaw. Which end do you sit on?

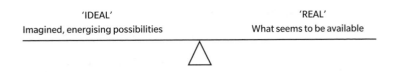

'IDEAL'	'REAL'
Imagined, energising possibilities	What seems to be available

In a typical job search, people start out feeling optimistic, but a few rejections can easily push them towards the right-hand side. Surely it's better to be realistic? Yes, if you make choices based on evidence. But how many people influencing you really know what is 'real' about today's world of work, understand where new roles are being created or what skills employers really need? When family and friends pass you job advertisements and say, 'Focus on the real world' (see Chapter 11), they mean obvious, uninspiring roles which are easy to get. You end up applying for a job you can do in your sleep.

Let's be clear, there are problems at both ends of the seesaw. The ideal end might limit you to roles which are rare, so you only push on doors likely to stay closed. Advice which says, 'Just dream the dream' or 'You can be anything you want to be', boosts you for a while, but early knockbacks can push you deep into 'realistic' mode. Are you looking at a likely career path (something you can do something about), or a comforting daydream?

Settling for 'realistic' options has a major impact on energy levels – you end up making uninspired job applications and saying little in an interview which anyone will remember. You sleepwalk your way into a role in default mode (see Exercise 1.1).

Without a spark of idealism you lack motivation to experiment and turn curiosity into enquiry. The 'ideal' end of the spectrum nudges you outside your comfort zone towards unexpected conversations and discoveries.

Where would you place yourself on the ideal/real range below?

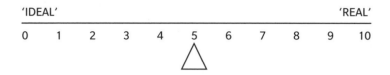

'IDEAL'										'REAL'
0	1	2	3	4	5	6	7	8	9	10

What does your score say about your thinking? A score around 4 seems to offer a useful balance between enthusiasm and pragmatism. Forget the bad press that 'ideal' receives, and all those people who tell you not to waste time looking for your dream role. You're looking for the right mix of elements in a job, not a perfect match.

Exercise 3.3
Your jigsaw job

This exercise allows you to see the component parts of your ideal job without getting locked into a job title.

Imagine that you buy a jigsaw puzzle from a charity shop. The puzzle is in a plastic bag with no box, picture or title. You probably begin with the edges, not worrying whether the final picture will show a cottage, a seascape or a kitten.

Now imagine you're in a role which is fulfilling. Don't worry what the job is called. Start by imagining what it feels like to be in this role which you enjoy. You've been in the role for at least 12 months and it's still stimulating.

The first question is around location and setting. Imagining yourself in this 'virtual' role, what do you see around you?

Look at the example below to build up your own jigsaw job. What are your answers to the topics in the left-hand column?

Topic	Example response
Location, setting	Urban. Aesthetically pleasing building in multicultural centre. Good light. The role involves travel and meeting people
Hours	The opportunity to work from home a couple of days a week
People	A role where I have a mentor. Trusting, cooperative environment. To be part of an enthusiastic, smart team – sharing ideas, thinking collectively
The way I manage other people	More a mentor than a supervisor. I like people I can rely on to do the job without being chased
The way I am managed	My boss is direct, honest, sees my potential. Keeps me on the straight and narrow but gives me freedom to perform tasks in my own way
Skills I use	Being the face of the organisation. Liaising, explaining; translating complex ideas into straightforward terms. Communicating/influencing. Using creative and analytical thinking
Problems	Trying to help people with their problems. Completing work on time
Challenges	Competition: something to drive me. The job is testing/stretching. Learning about managing/leadership
Values expressed	Strong ethos. Clear sense of purpose/meaning
Likely/attractive outcomes include	Getting a team result. Bringing the best out of people. Delighting the client

Topic	Example response
General details	A firm that's large enough to help me grow, small enough to support people
The job will be rewarding because . . .	I will be achieving something. It will be fun
How work contributes to my life outside work	Comfortable lifestyle. Health. Well-being
Work will allow time and energy for me to do these things outside work	Spending time with family and friends. Enjoying the theatre and cultural events again

- -

Working towards a healthy deal

The Taylor Report (2017) focused on *good work*. The idea isn't new; economists have known for centuries that certain kinds of work are intrinsically fulfilling, others draining. There are many modern indicators of what 'good' looks like, including not just the safety, health and well-being of workers, but also job security, workers' rights, fair wages, lifelong learning, career development and work–life balance.

Considering good work means thinking about what work gives you and what it takes away. How much energy do you have left after work? How much time does work leave for other things that matter to you? This book asks you to think about *dream jobs* in order to see what attracts you to *real jobs*. 'Compromise' doesn't mean defeat:

**All work is a deal
between what you want out of life
and what an employer
wants out of you.**

Aim for 70 per cent

Aiming for the perfect job is a '100 per cent or nothing' approach. It sounds ambitious, but in fact guarantees a quiet life. You've set the bar so high you have a great excuse to stop looking. Work is about deal making, and *good enough* works just fine.

Analysing a potential deal is straightforward. Start by achieving maximum clarity about what *you* want to get out of work, using the breadth of tools in this book. Next, learn how to scrutinise roles, digging much deeper than the job description. Information interviews (see Chapter 13) help you unearth real expectations and job content. When you understand what the role is really like (it will usually involve at least one conversation with someone who knows the organisation well), measure the overlap:

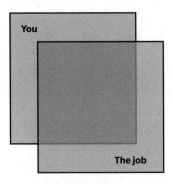

If your research is accurate, and you identify an overlap of around 70 per cent, the job is a good match. You'll feel engaged for around 3½ days out of 5, which is plenty – every job has its routine aspects. If the overlap is closer to 50 per cent, the role may be an acceptable stepping stone. If less, watch out.

Bringing energy from the past into the present

Exploring and deal making require energy. Energy can come from other people, but also from the way you choose to place your attention. Remembering a time at work when things went brilliantly will fill you with a positive buzz. It's worth reliving moments like this.

In contrast, you can lock your attention onto negative ideas. If you persuade yourself there's not much out there you can do, that dark picture absorbs energy very quickly. If you feel the glass is half empty, you believe it. You explore less, you have less to say. You assume there's nothing around the next corner. Your attention is fixed on absence. You catastrophise after setbacks.

Try something different. *Choose* to see possibilities, not gaps – choices, not limits. Choose to see the glass as half full. Soon you see abundance – and you see it everywhere. I love the strapline used by the Australasian car hire firm Jucy: 'The glass is half full – and the other half was delicious.'

Learn how to bottle energy from your past. Look at times when you felt fully engaged. This might be at work, or outside work. Notice how you become animated when you talk about these moments. That's energy from the past which you can capture and reuse, bringing it into the present whenever you write or talk about your work history. Communicate this energy – practise using energised language when you talk about work, and in a CV start using active verbs (e.g. 'led', 'reorganised', 'created'). At interview, rather than just mentioning a skill, start a sentence, 'I really enjoyed. . . '. Above-average candidates don't just tell stories, they tell stories which bring energy from the original experience into the room (see Chapter 15).

Energy helps at every stage of the process. Look for organisations, sectors, products and roles that spark your curiosity; this energy feeds a hunger to find out more. If you talk in a lively way about your interests and discoveries, people remember you. If you're conducting a springboard conversation (see Chapter 13), your enthusiasm is reason enough to pass you along.

Testing ideas

Finding out, following your enthusiasm, costs very little. Deciding to look is one of the smallest yet most powerful decisions you'll ever make. All you need is curiosity, and a plan. What does Day 1 of your plan look like? Here's a big clue: Your breakthrough probably has a 5 per cent likelihood of happening as a result of reading or thinking, and a 95 per cent likelihood of occurring as a result of another human. Someone you already know, possibly – or someone you meet in the next three months. The first step is usually a conversation – for encouragement, clarification, ideas, road-testing language or help to map what's out there.

Start with people who will talk to you without hesitation, even if they are not obviously connected to sectors you want to investigate. Experiment with springboard conversations (see Chapter 13), or through 'shift projects' (see below).

Shift projects

Richard Alderson, founder of Careershifters

When I was desperately unhappy in my job, I did what I thought were the sensible things to do: I spoke to recruiters, I read career books, I did psychometric tests, I made lists and I did a lot of analysis.

None of these led me to a definitive answer as to what else I could do. Instead, I felt like I was going round and round in circles.

It was only when I started to take actions in the outside world – meeting new people, doing new things and stepping into new environments – that clarity started to emerge.

Why? Because, only in hindsight did I realise that I was trapped in my own reality bubble – the people, places and perspectives that made up my world. If the answer to my career change challenge lay in the world around me, I would have found it. Instead, I needed to break out of my bubble.

Taking real-world actions did this for me. Not only did they reveal new career options (indeed the role I shifted into was in a field I previously didn't even know existed), but they also allowed me to test these options to see which ones were viable.

This action-learning approach has become the core of the methodology that we've used at Careershifters to help more than 15,000 people on their journeys to finding more fulfilling work.

It's based around the concept of **shift projects**.

Shift projects are short experiments designed to discover or test career ideas. They have three essential qualities: they're action-based experiences (talking to people or trying things out – scrolling through Google doesn't count); they're quick, so you don't waste time on things that aren't right (think a few hours to a few weeks max.) and they're carried out with a light, curious approach (because many will be dead ends).

The following are examples of shift projects our clients have run:

- Alex, a project manager, volunteered part-time for a tech start-up to see how it would feel compared to the large corporate environment he'd come from.
- Michelle, an administrator, went to a culinary exhibition to explore how she could potentially turn her love of food into paid work.

- Simon, an IT consultant, started a mindfulness group in his company to test whether he could potentially grow it into a business.
- Annika, a researcher, met with an entrepreneur pioneering more sustainability in the interior design industry to learn more about her work.

In the initial stages of a career change, shift projects reconnect you with the things that energise you, enable you to see new career possibilities and help you get clearer about what you really want. Critically, you often need to start running them without an initial direction, which can feel counter-intuitive.

In the later stages of a career change, shift projects enable you to test and validate different specific career paths – helping you get clear on what other options would be viable, before you need to take unnecessary financial risks.

You can read more about shift projects at www.careershifters.org.

Career Change Test

Careershifters have designed a Career Change Test exclusively for readers of *How to Get a Job You Love*. This short, free assessment gives you a personalised report designed to help you understand what career stage you're at and how ready you are to make a successful career shift.

Take your test, free of charge, at www.careershifters.org/htg-test.

chapter 4

Thinking, deciding and getting on with it

'If you can dream – and not make dreams your master;

If you can think – and not make thoughts your aim. . . '

Rudyard Kipling (1910)

This chapter helps you to

- break out of A to Z thinking and become an ideas factory;
- learn to be less passive and more experimental;
- distinguish between dreams and goals;
- understand the areas of work that might attract you;
- believe and behave differently.

I can't decide what kind of career I want . . .

You might be wondering, 'If I was going to do something different, what would it be?' The key question is, *'How are you going to find out?'* People secretly believe that the answer will come along if they take a test, read a book or just sit at home with the curtains closed and think really, really hard.

You might be trying to solve the puzzle using *A to Z thinking* – trying to follow a logical, straight-line path from problem to solution. This kind of thinking works fine when you start with a single goal in mind. However, when you need to navigate unknown territory, imagination and curiosity give you better results. Changing career requires new kinds of thinking. A key part of new thinking is *reframing* – seeing things you think you know from an entirely new perspective. A to Z thinking just takes you where you plan to go. Curiosity shows you a thousand routes.

Marilyn Ferguson (1987) reminds us that change comes from within: 'No one can persuade another to change. Each of us guards a gate of change that can only be opened from the inside. We cannot open the gate of another either by argument or by emotional appeal.' Push your brain into a new gear. Avoid dismissing ideas by saying 'yes, but' and thinking in circles (see Chapter 2).

Become an ideas factory, hungry to discover jobs and organisations you've never heard of. Turn an idea into an enquiry rather than finding evidence to shoot it down. Every time you find an idea you like, do something with it. Don't get lost in Google – other people are the best way to map new territory. Seize on the energy that feeling curious provides – dig deeper, find someone who can answer your next question. Reframing is about trying on ideas and seeing what doors they open.

Ideas factory

Suggestions for building career ideas:

- Allow yourself to generate a range of ideas, without self-criticism.
- If you feel your brain is overloaded, do something entirely different – go to the gym, watch a movie, cook. Putting your brain in a new gear is often a great way of generating ideas.
- When a new idea hits you, don't dismiss it as daydreaming. Test it out.
- Write out ideas on postcards or Post-it notes. Look for connections. See what happens when you combine two or three ideas. Prioritise your ideas so you know what to give maximum focus.
- Dig deeper into sectors (see Chapter 9).
- Turn your idea upside down. For example, you may be interested in child development because you are interested in the way young people grow. Turning that upside down might lead you to thinking about the effects of ageing.
- *Do* something with every career idea – turn it into a piece of research or a conversation.

Be more experimental

Enjoy the freedom of exploration and discovery; put your decision-hungry brain on hold. You don't have to make a big life decision yet.

You need to make a choice, though – to keep looking, and to keep asking questions.

Think of this process as spinning half a dozen plates in the air, giving each plate just a little extra spin every day. Don't be put off if you don't get amazing results overnight. Most experiments don't lead to instant success; every invention builds on a history of failed attempts. Resist pressure from friends, family and professional contacts to do the next obvious thing (see Exercise 1.1).

Since some of this involves imagination, you might be tempted to hide behind the statement 'I'm not a creative person'. Let's establish a ground rule. We're all creative in some way. We are all capable of inventing creative solutions to life's varied problems, such as taking children in opposite directions in one car, paying this week's bills with next week's money, caring for three or four difficult children at their most unpleasant or making dinner out of six things in the cupboard. We are all capable of flexible, creative thinking. We have to be; that's how humans have survived.

You don't need to be ultra-creative, or brave, to explore – especially when you find easy ways of setting up conversations (see Chapter 13). Look for the next door to open, the next conversation to move you forward. The most important work you put into your career isn't about CV writing or interview preparation, it's about *learning to think differently*. In its simplest form this means ignoring 'yes, but', and saying 'what else should I look at. . . how can I find out more?'

Shift your language

Try a change of vocabulary. Practise a register shift, from no to **yes**.

The language of NO	The language of YES
It'll never work	Let's look at alternatives
It's how I am; I was born that way	I'll try a different approach
It's against the rules	I'll invent a new rulebook

The language of NO	The language of YES
It's not for me	I need to find out more
I'm forced to	I will choose
In the real world . . .	I make my world real by . . .
Another mistake . . .	How interesting . . .
If only . . .	Let's try . . .
I need to be certain	I want to discover more
Never	It's all experimental

Distinguish between goals and dreams

You might have a daydream job. Maybe running a small and highly profitable beach bar somewhere where the weather is glorious and the hours are short. These dreams are fun, keeping us warm on winter nights, and they are also entirely safe – you never have to do anything about them. Daydreams are for entertainment and distraction from routine. A goal is very different – you need to do something about it.

Some people believe that success arrives by setting adventurous goals and sticking to them with fanatical commitment. In his book *59 Seconds*, Richard Wiseman debunks some of these goal-setting myths; for example, the idea that if you write down big goals they are more likely to happen (there is no research data to support this). However, there is evidence to suggest that short-term goal setting is effective. If you break tasks down into mini-objectives, you're more likely to make progress – especially if you reward yourself for completing each stage, which only happens if you complete step one.

This can sound a little overprocessed. Don't lose sight of the original fascination you experienced when you came across an idea for exploration. If something draws you, it gives you the energy to step outside your comfort zone and make something happen. Most of the time, real discovery means finding someone to talk to.

Make it so

How do you keep exploring? Do it as if all jobs pay the same. Do it as if all doors will open if you ask. Do it as if it really matters to you – because it probably does.

Do it as if you were doing it for somebody else. Imagine a friend offers you a thousand pounds a month to spend finding her ideal career. If you took the task on, you wouldn't go back every five minutes saying, 'You wouldn't like this' or 'This won't work' – yet, this is what you do for yourself. If you were doing it for someone else, you'd keep looking for angles, keep finding connections, keep generating ideas without trashing them. Start by generating ideas for work sectors that look interesting, decide who to reach out to first, then press the button.

In various incarnations of *Star Trek*, Jean-Luc Picard (played by the inimitable Patrick Stewart) executes commands with three plain words: *Make it so*. You really do know what the first step is, so just begin. Think in terms of pilot schemes and experiments – low-risk ways of getting things moving. Move on from 'what if' to 'how could I make this work?' If a sector looks interesting, work out some of the practicalities of landing in it. Learn something, volunteer, shadow someone at work, start a 'side hustle'. Short-term or temporary employment can sometimes help to provide a useful 'laboratory' for your career plans. Sometimes the ground rule for experiment is: 'Don't think, just leap'.

Exercise 4.1
Work themes

- -

'Starting from the inside' means putting together a recipe for the kind of job that will work for you. One simple index of whether the job will work well for you is to think about the big themes that characterise the work.

Scoring: Give each work theme a score between 1 and 5, where 1 = little interest, 3 = moderate interest, 5 = high interest.

| Creativity | Your preferred work is mainly about working imaginatively with ideas or designs; for example, the arts, performing, creative writing, visual design, lateral thinking, business creativity, adapting ideas, coming up with new ideas, challenging assumptions. |
| Score: | |

| Hands on | Your preference is working hands on, engaging with the physical world; for example, building, shaping, cooking, craft, DIY, working with animals, plants, machines, vehicles, sports, physical fitness, physiotherapy, or working outdoors. |
| Score: | |

| Influence | Your preference is working with and through other people and will involve: leadership, management, changing organisations, setting up a new business or department, inventing, reorganising, shaping teams, driving others, influencing, persuading, motivating, selling, getting results. |
| Score: | |

| Information | Your ideal work is mainly about working with information; for example, analysing, cataloguing, gathering, planning, managing projects, researching, tracking down information, working with numbers or accounts, making the most of computers. |
| Score: | |

| Systems | You are most attracted to working with systems; for example, processes, quality control, continuous improvement, legal processes, procedures, bookkeeping, record-keeping, database management, health and safety. |
| Score: | |

People	Your preference is for working with people; for example, training, teaching, coaching, mentoring, developing, caring, nursing, nurturing, healing.
Score:	

Look at your top three work themes. For example, if your top three themes are *Creativity*, *People* and *Hands on*, you'll want to think about the kind of work that mixes all three – you might enjoy a role that involves creative teams, inventing new rules occasionally, achieving tangible results. Your work theme combination is unique to you, because it also draws upon your knowledge, values and experience.

- -

Ruts and channels

You might feel you're 'stuck in a rut' – uninspired by the same old, same old. The worst kind of rut is the *velvet rut*: you hate being in it, but it's too comfortable to climb out of. Ruts stay ruts because you get stuck in your thinking. You know that something needs to change, but it seems like hard work, or unimaginable. Your secret plan is to wait until someone or something pushes you out. Passive behaviour is widespread.

What's needed is a new angle. Define the problem in terms of your future emotional state. If you feel bored or dispirited now, how would you like to feel in the future? In a year's time? What changes would friends and family notice in you if you made this change? What first step can you take tomorrow?

Careers are often shaped by passively accepted assumptions. The fashion designer Ozwald Boateng was interviewed on BBC Radio 4's *Midweek* programme in March 2012. He recalled that his father's career advice was that if something 'came easy' to Ozwald, he should stick at it. So he did, switching from a course in computer studies to fashion. His father quickly said that this wasn't what he had in mind, but Boateng stuck at it and has built a highly successful international business. Your talents are not always evident until you discover them, but if you find something you do well that 'comes easy', where you can shine naturally, that's a great place to start.

One of the reasons people remain stuck in uninspiring work is that we are adaptable. Humans live in climates ranging from Arctic chill to desert heat. We can survive in the most unhealthy, difficult conditions; families can work, raise children and live good lives even under the most brutal political regimes. Perhaps because of this talent for survival, many have the capacity to do something that modern society finds odd and most of history saw as the norm. We can hold down an uninspiring job for decades. Given a world of choice, the fact that you *can* doesn't mean that you *should*.

Behaviour and belief

The greatest barriers between you and an inspired career are not in the marketplace, but in your brain. Let's adopt two rules. They don't sit happily together, which is what makes them interesting.

Rule 1: **behaviour follows belief**. We know this is true. If you believe you can do something, you do it well and talk about strengths with credibility. If you *feel* confident and in control, that's how you act. So, believe in what you can do a little bit more. Believe in your brain's ability to create ideas, research possibilities and make connections – and you'll do all of these things. Believe in the process of change, and believe that you have stories worth hearing.

The creative mind can hold contradictory ideas at the same time. So to Rule 2: **belief follows behaviour**. Behaving differently makes us think differently. It's sometimes easier to *act your way into a new way of thinking* than to *think your way into a new way of acting*. Try it. Next time you go into a stressful meeting, act as if you are in control. Speak more slowly and carefully. Sit still, breathe deeply. Rehearse the opening moments of a public presentation so you walk, stand and talk as if you have the audience's attention. Begin a job interview with the composure of someone already winning in the role.

Walk the walk, talk the talk, and something happens – you act your way into a new way of believing in yourself. That's why it's easier to show authority if you are dressed professionally, and why people are more assertive on the phone when they stand up. If you act as if you are already confident, you become it – quicker than you imagine. Richard Rohr (1999) wrote, 'We do not think ourselves into new ways of living, we live ourselves into new ways of thinking.'

Exercise 4.2
Getting your story in focus

- -

As you become focused on what you want to do next, you need a short story capturing how your career brings you to this point. Completing this exercise will give you more than you need.

Make notes in the right-hand column about what you will say.

Summary phrase This might be a generic job title (e.g. *communications professional*) or a short phrase	I am/Essentially what I do is. . .

Relevant background A brief reference to your background	I started in. . .

Key strengths Relevant to where you want to go next. Talk briefly about skills, knowledge or working style	What I enjoy doing. . .

What attracts me to this kind of role Short statements matching a few parts of your background to a sector or role	I find this kind of role exciting because . . .

Plans for experiment Things you'd like to start, develop or complete in the role	I'd like an opportunity to. . .

Impact What results you'd hope to achieve in the first six months	I'd like to achieve . . .

People outcomes You might talk about this rather than Impact	I'd like to make people feel. . .

One client's completed Exercise 4.2 looked like this: **Summary phrase:** *I write stories about financial markets for institutions, general consumers and private investors.* **Relevant background:** *I started in consumer research but became really interested in writing influential journalism.* **Key strengths:** *I really enjoy talking to market leaders and media contacts and understanding key issues.* **What attracts me to this kind of role:** *The challenge of providing different messages for different audiences.* **Plans for experiment:** *I'd really like the opportunity to take corporate bulletins and annual reports online and make them more interactive. . .* **Impact:** *I want to get much more out of media contacts. . .* **People outcomes:** *I want people to feel that investment isn't a mystery. . . .*

As you come closer to deciding what you are looking for, you will ask questions, but people will also show curiosity about you, and what you're looking for. This is a great opportunity to give a positive, memorable answer which helps people understand your career story, one which explains why you fit the kinds of role you now have firmly in your sights. Note how the structure of Exercise 4.2 moves from past to present, making firm connections between your experience and the impact you will have in a role.

Tariq, NHS Chief Executive

Tariq had enjoyed a career in IT and communications, but had a strong motivation to 'give something back' by a move into the health sector.

A strategy developed: 'I learned the power of networking to explore my target sector. This took me way outside my comfort zone. I'd been really confident in the past but was very reluctant to approach people I didn't know.'

At first he found it difficult to make his background seem relevant until he learned how to make the most of his transferable skills. He even learned how to show that his original history degree, focused on leaders and empires, 'prepared me well for organisational politics'.

Contacts in the health sector pointed to the value of 'even short bursts of experience'. The turning point came with a rejection letter following a job application. Tariq turned it into a conversation about the hospital's needs and into a breakthrough short-term assignment.

Tariq focused on building a CV managing change in a range of health authorities, and quickly became appointed as the turnaround director for a high-profile trust.

Having started with recruiters telling him that this kind of move was virtually impossible, Tariq became chief executive of a health trust, competing with applicants with far more health sector experience.

Looking back at the process, Tariq describes it as a mix of 'creative thinking and mad courage'.

chapter 5

What drives you?

'And nothing to look backward
to with pride,

And nothing to look forward
to with hope.'

Robert Frost (1914a)

This chapter offers opportunities to

- look at workplace turn-offs;
- think about the part money plays in your career;
- identify what motivates you;
- discover your career hot buttons.

Turn-ons and turn-offs at work

Most roles are interesting when you start, simply because they're new. As jobs become familiar, sometimes repetitive, motivation can fade – which is one reason employee engagement is a continuing problem for organisations (see Chapter 1). Employers understand what prompts someone to take a job, but less about long-term motivation.

Go back to Exercise 3.1. What might you describe as good, bad or just plain awful in your current job? Categorise your dissatisfactions: physical work environment, location, colleagues you work with, management style, lack of independence, status, recognition, people, tasks, variety, values of the organisation, and so on. Think about elements in a job that demotivate you – make you feel that your effort is wasted or unappreciated, or tasks that seem meaningless.

When talking about why they're leaving a job, people often use shorthand: 'I hate everything about it.' There is usually at least one thing they enjoyed, apart from going home. Think about a job you've disliked. What one thing made the day more bearable? What moments, interactions or tasks seemed more interesting?

Think more broadly reflecting on everything you've done which is work related, including voluntary roles. What has been your most enjoyable role or project so far, and why? What parts of *any* job keep you interested, excited, focused? These factors may be about results ('The customers were great but my boss was awful'), or context ('I had a great bunch of colleagues').

Exercise 5.1
The 3-minute motivation checklist

- -

What motivates you to get up in the morning and go to work?

You have £20 to spend on yourself. Spend it in the table below on the things that really motivate you in work. You might spend £20 on one item, or spread your money around (don't use units smaller than £1).

	Motivating factor	£s
1	**Status** My worth is recognised in my job title/pay level/responsibilities . . .	
2	**Recognition** I am recognised for my skills and contribution.	
3	**Feedback** I am told when I am doing a good job.	
4	**Skills balance** My opportunities and skills are well matched.	
5	**Challenge** I like to take on new projects and problems.	
6	**Leadership** I enjoy opportunities to lead others.	
7	**Personal development** I have continuing opportunities to learn and grow.	
8	**Variety** My work is varied and interesting.	
9	**Responsibility** I am responsible for important people or projects.	
10	**Intellectual challenge** I like to be stretched and to improve my expertise.	

➤

	Motivating factor	£s
11	**Independence/freedom** I have some control over how I spend my time at work and where I go.	
12	**Fun** I spend time in lively, companionable groups that enjoy working together.	
13	**Team membership** I enjoy being part of an active, supportive team.	
14	**Making a difference/contributing** I can see what my contribution adds to the whole process.	
15	**Helping others** My work contributes to others, or to society as a whole.	
16	**Meaning and fulfilment** My work has purpose and seems meaningful.	
17	**Security** Knowing what I will be doing and earning in a year's time matters to me.	
18	**Earnings now** I feel reasonably well paid.	
19	**Earnings potential** My earnings will probably increase significantly in the future.	
20	**Fringe benefits** The job has interesting side benefits.	

Building on the 3-minute motivation checklist

Review the motivators you have chosen. How different would this list have looked five or ten years ago? What motivates us can change a great deal.

This exercise has been used more than any other in this book – with thousands of clients, workshop and conference delegates. Feedback reveals different ways it helps people making a career change:

- Look at your higher scoring items. How many of them match the job you're in at the moment? What motivators are missing from your current role? What difference would it make to you if more of them were present?
- When have you felt really motivated? Think of concrete examples: projects, occasions, teams.
- What demotivates you in work?
- If you have put scores against rows 18–20, where would you reallocate those £s if the money was right in a new role?
- Use this sheet as a template for exploration. What roles would provide a good match to your strongest motivators?
- Use this sheet as a checklist if you're offered a job. What key ingredients would you like to have in your next role (you won't get them all – see the 70 per cent overlap on p. 34).
- Look at where you have allocated £2 or more. Think about times at work when those motivators were matched. Next, find someone to talk to about these experiences. Look at the way you become more energised as you tell these stories – build on them as you prepare for interviews.

Isn't money the main motivator?

'What motivates you?' Recruitment consultants ask this question, and the answer they usually hear is 'money'. It's convenient shorthand (and something you're guessing a recruiter wants to hear – code for 'ambitious').

In fact, you may not be motivated by money at all. Daniel Pink (2009) throws fascinating light on motivation. He argues that financial incentives rarely make workers more creative or productive, but motivation can be maintained in the long term (even if the job isn't terribly exciting) when workers experience *autonomy* (some choice about how the job is done), *mastery* (continued skill improvement) and *purpose* (the job contributes to outcomes worth achieving).

Psychologists confirm that money is a weak motivator, but a powerful *de*motivator. We are usually more influenced by loss than gain. For example, finding £20 on the street may cheer you up briefly, but losing £5 from your pocket can ruin your day. A pay raise seems to have only a short-term effect on engagement and productivity. High pay helps to retain workers, but doesn't necessarily keep them engaged. If you receive a new year pay raise, you will probably have forgotten about it within a month, but if you receive a pay cut, it will bother you every time your salary hits your bank account, and every time you speculate about what your friends are earning. Feeling underpaid has a long-term demotivating effect, especially where you feel your work is not appreciated.

How do you know what you are worth? I have seen individuals interviewed for £40,000 and £80,000 jobs in the same week, with little real difference in responsibility or complexity. Markets often do very odd things with salaries. Have you ever calculated what you really cost your employer, including overheads, cost of hire and training? It's around twice your salary. What have you contributed in return – or what could you do if you had more freedom? How far do colleagues notice the value you add? How much of your contribution is invisible, unacknowledged?

When asked, 'How much money would you need so you feel you have *enough*?', people often name a figure double their present income, whether they earn £15,000 or £150,000 a year – which shows that a great deal of this is about feeling, not your bank balance. Some career books ask you to work out the minimum you need to pay all your bills and to eat. Unfortunately, far too many people confuse this figure with what they are worth.

You might assume that to make a career change you'll need to take a pay cut. That may sometimes be true, but don't assume it's an automatic requirement. It's better to work out what the market normally pays for a role, and then to work out what you might be able to offer to put yourself in the top end of a pay range (see Chapter 15 on negotiating pay).

Take time using this book to see how your skills and knowledge add value, in concrete terms. Where have you introduced cost savings? Where have you brought in or protected income streams? How much would it cost to replace you with consultants or agency contractors? Be clear of the value you add in hard financial terms. Now think ahead. Assuming you keep motivated, keep learning and move forward in your career, what annual earnings do you want to achieve in five years' time?

When people under or overestimate their earning power, this usually means they don't understand the market they're aiming at. Think about how you can find out more about your market value. What first steps can you take to find a job that pays reasonably well and motivates you for more than a few months?

For a small proportion of people, having the capacity to earn large amounts is like an internal game, constantly challenging. Most of us want to feel we're paid what we are worth. Pay is rarely the single motivator when people leave one job for another – unless someone is seriously underpaid. Sometimes workers take a pay cut for the right role or a change of scene. Once pay issues are resolved, deeper 'hot buttons' kick in (see later in this chapter) – e.g. being respected for your expertise, seeing the job through to the finish, making a difference, having great colleagues, or opportunities to keep learning – some of the reasons it feels worth getting out of bed for on a cold Monday morning.

Having explored your motivation quickly, let's go into career drivers in more depth.

Exercise 5.2
Career hot buttons

- -

Read all the questions below and then circle the overall score you
feel is right in each category. Use the full scale rather than bunch all
your scores in the middle.

---

1 Financial rewards

- How important is the money, really? How much would you be
  re-energised if your salary increased by 10 per cent? 20 per
  cent? How long would that feeling last?
- How motivated are you by financial rewards such as bonus
  payments?
- If you could do more of the great things about your job and
  fewer of the dull things, would you be just as happy with less
  money?
- When you're at a party and listening to people talk about their
  jobs, how much do you think about what they earn? How much
  does it matter to you if you feel you're earning less than your
  peers?

Financial rewards are:

1	2	3	4	5	6	7	8	9	10
Unimportant			Moderately important				Very important		

---

2 Influence

- How much do you enjoy leadership and persuasion (high influence)?
- How much control do you like to have over people, situations,
  problems?
- How much does it trouble you when you have little influence
  over decisions?
- Do you prefer to be in charge (high influence) or are you happy
  to follow a good leader (low influence)?
- How much do you like to have a say in change?

Influence is:

1	2	3	4	5	6	7	8	9	10
Unimportant			Moderately important				Very important		

3 Expert

- How important is the feeling of being knowledgeable, skilled, an expert?
- Are you generally happy knowing a lot about one focused area of knowledge?
- Do you enjoy a reputation as a specialist (high expertise) or are you flexible enough to take on a wide range of tasks (low expertise)?
- Do you enjoy it when others seek you out to ask for your advice or specialist knowledge?

Being an expert is:

1	2	3	4	5	6	7	8	9	10
Unimportant			Moderately important				Very important		

4 Independence

- How far do you prefer a mentor to a supervisor?
- Are you a self-starter? How much do you like to set your own deadlines?
- How much control do you like over how you will allocate your time in achieving a task?
- How much does it matter to you that you decide how you spend your time?
- Do you like to have control over what you do (high independence) or are you happy to accept intelligent supervision (mid to low independence)?

Independence at work is:

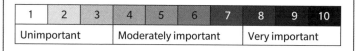

1	2	3	4	5	6	7	8	9	10
Unimportant			Moderately important				Very important		

5 Relationships

- How important are close relationships at work to you?
- Do you tend to make friends through work?
- Are you more productive working in a team (high relationships) or quietly on your own (low relationships)?
- How important is it to you to trust and be trusted?

Relationships at work are:

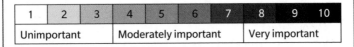

1	2	3	4	5	6	7	8	9	10
Unimportant			Moderately important				Very important		

6 Security

- How far do you need to feel you are financially secure?
- How much does it matter that you have a nest egg, a safety barrier – a cushion against ill fortune (high security)?
- How happy are you to take on risks of varying kinds (low security)?
- How important is it to you that you know what you will be doing next year?

Security in work is:

1	2	3	4	5	6	7	8	9	10
Unimportant			Moderately important				Very important		

7 Status

- How much does your reputation matter to you?
- How important is it to you to have your skills recognised by your colleagues, your profession, your community (high status)?
- How far are you happy to work in the background, getting the job done, not minding who gets the credit (low status)?
- How important is it to you to have a job title that reflects the level and impact of your job?

Status is:

1	2	3	4	5	6	7	8	9	10
Unimportant			Moderately important				Very important		

8 Meaning and fulfilment

- How strongly do you feel about the value your work adds to your community or society as a whole?
- How aware are you of the damage your work might be doing to others, or to the environment?
- Do you hear yourself saying that your work should be *meaning-ful* or *purposeful*?
- Are you happy to seek meaning outside your working life?

My search for meaning through work is:

1	2	3	4	5	6	7	8	9	10
Unimportant			Moderately important				Very important		

9 Imagination

- Are you good at discovering new ideas, new ways of doing things?
- Do you prefer to let others come up with ideas while you do the detailed planning?
- Do you prefer to follow a system or set of rules (low imagination)?
- Or do you like to invent new solutions to problems (high imagination)?

Using imagination at work is:

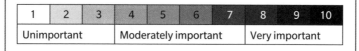

1	2	3	4	5	6	7	8	9	10
Unimportant			Moderately important				Very important		

Career hot buttons: Total scores and rank order

Career hot buttons	Total	Rank order
1 Financial rewards		
2 Influence		
3 Expert		
4 Independence		
5 Relationships		
6 Security		
7 Status		
8 Meaning and fulfilment		
9 Imagination		

Now list your top 4 hot buttons below, in rank order. This may be straightforward, but you may find you have items with the same score. If so, make a decision about what matters most in a job. (For example, if your scores for **Influence** and **Status** are the same, ask yourself: 'Would I prefer a job where influence is *marginally* more important than status?')

My top 4 career hot buttons
1
2
3
4

Building on your career hot buttons

Look at your top 4 hot buttons, and think about your present or most recent role. How many of these buttons were satisfied in the role? What's missing? What can you add to your present job, or seek in your next post? What blend of job ingredients might keep you motivated in the long term?

(Occupational psychologist Stuart Robertson has built on these hot buttons in the Career Motivation Indicator (careermotivation.co.uk).)

- -

Kathryn Jackson, leadership coach and founder of The Great Recharge

Kathryn writes: 'In 2006 I was working for a large UK retail bank as a resource manager. I enjoyed our task of building skills and capabilities within the leadership team. Then everything changed. Suddenly the most senior directors were constantly in meetings. The atmosphere shifted darkly; something big was on the horizon.

We could never have anticipated the Global Financial Crisis which decimated the UK banking industry. At first, I was angry about losing my job, and guilt ridden about not being able to help my team. . . then I got scared about how I was going to pay the bills, because financial companies weren't hiring.

I fell across *How to Get a Job You Love* and decided this might be a catalyst to find something different. Chapter by chapter things became clearer to me; the skills I enjoyed using, the difference I wanted to make, and the meaning I found in my work. Suddenly it hit me. The Job I Love was what the book was about – career coaching.

It was like a lightbulb going off, and the book's exercises helped build my plan. I used some of my redundancy payout to attend training, and the second half of my career began.'

chapter 6

Clarify your skills

'When love and skill work together,
expect a masterpiece.'

Charles Reade (1870)

This chapter helps you to

- understand how it's useful to consider skills separately from personality;
- map your hidden skills;
- communicate your motivated skills;
- understand what makes skills transferable;
- express skills and achievements as mini-narratives.

Skills – getting below the surface

Asking 'what's a skill?' might seem an unnecessary question until you look at those many CVs which start 'highly accomplished', 'motivated', 'enthusiastic'. These words describe aspects of personality and say nothing about skills. 'I am creative' is a statement about personality. 'I created. . .' begins to outline a skill. Skills are often described using verbs ('I managed'), personality characteristics in adjectives ('effective').

A skill is something you *do*. Personality is about *how* you do it. This distinction provides clarity when you want to communicate what you can do well. In reality, things blur; terms like 'strengths' or 'competencies' describe many things overlapping: attitude, mindset, working style, underpinning knowledge and skills. The picture starts to get fuzzy, and the key ingredient with maximum currency is your skill set.

A skill can be explained on three levels:

Simple statement	I am good at planning.
Skill plus context and details of the challenge	I planned a Zoom meeting for 200 people with two guest speakers, breakout rooms and a managed plenary session.
Skill plus details which indicate working style and outcomes	I planned the event – with attention to detail, anticipating likely problems – surpassing the attendance target and achieving above-average participant response scores.

A skill might be observable to others (organising, communicating, negotiating. . .) or something going on inside your head (planning, scripting, anticipating. . .).

Exercise 6.1
Skills catalogue in 10 steps

- -

Take a pad of paper. Use the prompts below to dig out some of your skills. Make sure you write down skills (e.g. organising, planning, negotiating), not aspects of personality (e.g. enthusiastic, reliable, calm).

1 Imagine it's Sunday night and you are looking forward to work tasks in the week ahead. What activities do you look forward to most?

2 Imagine you're having a brilliant day at work. If someone was following you round with a video camera, what activities would the recording show?

3 Think of the most enjoyable job you've ever done. What skills were you using?

4 Think of a project you look back on with pride. What skills were you using?

5 Think about a time when you surprised yourself by doing something you didn't know you were capable of doing. What was the skill you used?

6 Think about times when you have received praise for your work performance. What were the skills mentioned?

7 What skills come easily to you – what are you naturally good at?

8 Write down any other skills you are good at and you enjoy using.

9 Look at all the skills you have recorded in steps 1–8. If you could choose only one skill from this list, which one energises you most?

10 Finally, think about a day at work when you were entirely absorbed in what you were doing, time passed quickly, and you went home feeling a 'buzz'. Find someone to talk to about that day. Ask your listener to record every skill you describe or mention in your story. Add any new skills revealed to your list.

- -

See how the skills generated by Exercise 6.1 match certain categories. You may have skills connected with **information** (researching, managing data, analysing), or with **systems** (organising, planning, understanding processes and structures). Your skills might be connected with **imagination** (creating, designing, being innovative), or with **enterprise** (making new things happen, being an entrepreneur). Many have skills connected with **influencing people** (selling, communicating, negotiating, leading, driving change) or **developing people** (teaching, coaching, training, mentoring).

The skills you might not see

Wallpaper skills

Some of your skills are like wallpaper. If you hang new wallpaper at home, you're aware of it for a month or two, then you stop seeing it. It jumps back into focus when someone comments on your redecoration. Similarly, you use some skills so regularly they are invisible to you until someone brings them to your attention.

It's important to reclaim these skills, understand how effective they are and stop assuming that everyone has them. Even if some people do, they don't use them in the distinctive way you do.

Example: Sue's favourite activity is ballroom dancing but she leaves it off her CV because she feels it's irrelevant to work. One day, she heard of a college lecturer who taught business skills through ballroom dancing. Formal dancing teaches timing, responsiveness, leading and following, reading signals, anticipating change and paying attention to personal space. Sue realised that using these skills at work was what made her a brilliant PA.

Uncelebrated skills

You may have skills you use all the time, but you feel they have little or no value at work. Sometimes we describe them as 'hobby skills'. They could include horticulture, craft skills, fine hand-to-eye coordination, being good at crosswords, being a great sports coach. You might say, 'I talk to my friends about this all the time, but I don't see a way of putting it in my CV or talking about it at an interview'.

Example: Norma can't walk past a piece of fabric without touching it. She has a good eye for texture, colour and pattern, and for matching materials simply and cheaply to make a room look great. She has a knack of walking into a room and knowing how to make it look more appealing with a few simple changes. Recently she explored becoming a 'house doctor', offering low-cost design solutions to sell houses quickly.

Power skills

You've heard of 'soft' skills. The term comes from US military training, where 'hard', technical skills were about weapons and equipment and 'soft' skills were those influencing and communicating skills required by leaders. It's strange how the word 'soft' is now used to describe only very person-centred skills like listening – and how often people say that in business, hard skills are vital, soft skills are 'nice to have'.

Josh Bershin (2019) calls these interpersonal skills *power skills*, arguing that they are 'difficult to build, critical and take extreme effort to obtain'. He includes skills like teamwork, communication, innovation, collaboration, managing performance and ensuring the well-being of a workforce, arguing that 'hard' skills are largely technical, easy to learn and replace with automation, while 'power' skills are what really get results by shaping teams and organisations into more effective units.

Don't hide your interpersonal skills. Some of the most difficult outcomes happen because of well-crafted power skills – persuading, influencing, negotiating, motivating, inspiring and leading.

Example: Maureen's great skill is untangling messy personal situations. She helps people see things clearly, encouraging parties to put anger aside and seek common ground. Others see her oiling the wheels, mending broken relationships. She was entirely unaware of this until a friend said, 'Do you know what you do? You're the mortar between the bricks of our community.' She never gets the opportunity to use these skills at work, so she says nothing about them in her CV.

Unexplored skills

Think about skills you've always wanted to learn or develop, or just try out. Friends might hear you say, 'I always wanted to. . . ', or 'I wish I'd found the time to. . . '. Look for real career ideas in these fantasies. For example, if you like working with animals, find somewhere to volunteer. If you've always fancied being a long-distance lorry driver, look at retraining. If you've always dreamed of being a novelist, take a writing class, write the opening paragraph, read more novels. Want to be an MP? Become more active in your chosen political party. Do anything, but do something. Stretch yourself. Have a go. Shadow someone doing the job. Take a short course rather than a three-year degree. Try a shift project (see p. 36).

Example: Bill fixes computers and advises on software. He gives time freely to his local school. If he is invited to do anything with the children, it usually involves explaining something about IT. He's great at it: the best person the school can find. But his real interest is the natural world. What he really wants is to talk to the kids about pond life, and he thinks he'd be pretty good at it – if he had the opportunity.

Imagined skills

Some skills occupy our imagination. Think about the skills you admire in others, or times when you have watched someone performing a task and thought, 'I can see myself doing that'. When have you pictured yourself doing something you've never done before? How much of this imagination is a kind of longing? Often the best career challenge is to make sure skills don't stay imaginary.

Example: I sailed as a boy, not particularly well. I often dreamed about sailing again, and in the dream I usually felt I had no idea what I was doing. At the age of 40, I took up sailing again, and because I had practised sailing so often in my head, I was actually better at it. I've heard this phenomenon called 'learning to ski in the summer, learning to swim in the winter'. Sports research reveals that if you train by visualising events, the effect is almost as powerful as real experience. If that's true, then imagined skills are worth more than you think.

Motivated skills

Think about skills you use well. 'Use well' means moments when you complete a task satisfactorily, finish a project, please a customer. Now we'll think about skills you use well and *enjoy using* – motivated skills.

When you think about 'enjoy using', don't set the bar too high. Yes, you might find yourself in a state of *flow*, totally absorbed so that you lose track of time (see Csikszentmihalyi, 2008). On the other hand, you might just be enjoying the simple pleasure of using a skill effectively, creating results, making a small difference.

Think about the skills you perform well, but *don't enjoy using*. This reflection might reveal why certain roles haven't worked for you. You might feel you could do a task in your sleep or you've completed a task the same way too many times. You might feel, no matter how much you get paid to use the skill, that it really doesn't achieve anything important.

There are lots of clues pointing to motivated skills. Times when you felt really engaged. Times when you felt you were doing something that stretched you enjoyably, or an occasion when you surprised yourself in what you achieved. You enjoy telling stories about these experiences – moments when you felt completely yourself, in work or outside work. You look forward to using or improving these skills.

Think about times when you're getting ready for work, planning for the week ahead. This typically happens on a Sunday afternoon. You might be checking your diary, working out what you need to prepare in advance. How do you feel about work when you're doing that? What activities do you anticipate with dread? What do you visualise with enthusiasm? Think about tasks you look forward to performing. What exactly will you be doing?

Exercise 6.2
Motivated skills

- -

Look at skills you have identified in Exercise 6.1. Place them in the grid below.

Your motivated skills	Skills I love using	Skills I quite enjoy using	Skills I don't enjoy using much
Skills I perform well			
Skills I perform reasonably well but need to develop			
Skills I do not perform well			

Skills in the darker areas are those you should be using and developing. How many are you using in your current role? Put your top skills in your ideas grid (see Chapter 16).

- -

Finding the right words

Because you use skills every day, you might feel you know them well. However, many people seem uncertain or go silent when an interviewer asks, 'What are your top skills?' You might mention skills you hope will impress, or skills you used in a recent job. Colleagues at work may have affirmed some of your skills, but they aren't necessarily what you do best, just those valuable to the organisation. Even close friends may not see your full skill set or know what you enjoy doing.

Knowing what your skills are is easier than talking about them. One of the biggest barriers in career transition is the simplest – *learning to talk about yourself.* Many of us find it hard to talk about skills in a language we feel comfortable using. It can easily sound like empty bragging or an overstatement. It's easy to feel that your skills are not worth much. You might feel, deep down, that you don't really possess these skills and no one is interested in them.

The problem is that we've fallen for the idea that talking about skills is another form of selling. Go online and you'll find advice on crafting an 'elevator' pitch, a short summary beginning with a cheesy phrase like 'colleagues tell me I'm good at. . . '. At least half the population would run a mile before attempting this kind of self-promotion.

If you hate the idea of beginning a sentence with 'I am good at. . . ', *don't.* It won't come out well. It's infinitely easier to start a phrase beginning 'I get a buzz out of. . . ', or 'What I love doing is. . . ', or – even simpler – 'I really enjoy. . . ', then talk about an activity at work that energises you, for example, 'I really enjoy showing people how to get the best out of their smartphone camera' – simple, clear and not a hint of ego.

Claims and evidence

Anyone advising you on your CV will say, 'List your achievements.' The problem with the word 'achievements' is that we adopt demanding standards – assuming they need to be ultra-special to be worth mentioning. Your achievements don't have to be outstanding or rare events. You don't have to put in a world-class performance or break sales records. The achievements you write and talk about are the everyday stuff of getting things done – starting or finishing a project, hitting deadlines, coming in under budget, delighting the customer.

The skill is what you did, the achievement is the *outcome* – what happened because you were present. If the skill is valuable to you, convey its value to others.

Be aware that sometimes a reader's response to any skill you name might be, 'So what?' – especially if it's an obvious skill or one claimed by someone three rungs below your level. Otherwise, the reason you'll get a 'so what?' is that you've just named the skill, not told the story behind it. For example, *I am a good communicator* says almost nothing. What kind of communication? What kind of audience? Add brief details about the context and the outcome: 'I regularly had to communicate difficult messages to team members, keeping them motivated as well as informed – resulting in improved staff retention over a three-year period of organisational change.'

Evidence is neutral – what happened. Your task is to turn these facts into material which makes you sound employable. Turn basic evidence into polished achievement stories. Package each achievement into a simple, three-stage story:

The problem or challenge	Contribution – What I did	The outcome
My company needed to simplify its accounting system and save money.	Identified, researched and introduced an off-site central accounting function.	25 per cent savings, and the new accounts centre came online to budget and on deadline.

Create an evidence vault

Take a pad of paper. Don't look at your CV, just write down every example you can think of where you achieved a result. Don't apply filters ('is this worth recording?') and don't worry about the wording – use bullet points. Include things you've done outside work. Keep thinking – and ask for input from people who know you well. This is your evidence vault, your list of career highlights and achievements, so should run to more than two sheets of paper. Now look at all your bullet points. Decide on the top eight to ten you want to put in the spotlight on the first page of your CV, and the top one or two you might mention in conversation.

Making skills transferable

You have a lot of skills. They combine with your experience and mindset to create something distinctive. Most of your skills are *transferable*. What does this mean? Many job hunters believe that it's an employer's job to work out where their skills might fit. In reality busy hirers barely have time to discover your skills, never mind work out if they are useful.

A different question. What makes skills seem *non*-transferable? Because they don't offer an obvious connection to a role. They don't feel or sound relevant. Perhaps you are describing skills using language a listener can't understand, talking about things that don't seem to have any connection to the new context. The language might be technical jargon, or just unfamiliar.

What makes skills transferable? *You do*. Skills don't transfer themselves – they need to be translated – into terms a busy employer understands. In fact, go one step further. Skills become transferable when someone not only understands them, but *gets excited* about them. You don't just want people to notice your skills, you want them to say, 'We can use that skill here.'

You can also make better connections between the skills you love using *outside* work and what you do 9 to 5. Ask yourself, 'What's the best part of me my current employer isn't getting?'

Exercise 6.3
Skill movie trailer

- -

Think of a project or task (in work or outside work) that you are really proud of. Tell yourself the story: What was the challenge you faced? What did you do? What was the outcome?

Now think how you might make a 60-second movie trailer for this story using the prompts below.

What's the story?	What's the movie about? What would be a good title for your movie? Examples: *The day the system crashed. . .* *Speaking without notes. . .* *Thinking on my feet. . .*
Quests and monsters	What was the challenge? What problem were you solving? How big was it? Example: *My boss was on holiday and I had to deal with our biggest customer, who was fuming.*
Lead actor	How do you feature in the movie trailer? What part do you play in the story? Example: *I was thrown in the deep end.*

Zoom in on the action	What did you actually do? What high-energy words might describe what you were doing? Examples: *I got to grips with the problem. I pulled in resources and people.* *I made sure my voice was heard. I helped calm the situation.*
Plot summary	What happened because you were in this movie? What did you add? What difference did you make? Examples: *I was the only person who knew about X.* *I kept calm when others were panicking.* *I adapted the design quickly.*
Final frames	What did this tell you about challenges you love to face and skills you love to use? What would you do differently next time? Examples: *I learned that I can be creative in lots of situations.* *I learned that I enjoy having to think on my feet.* *I learned to be clear about the problem, find a solution and work out why things went wrong afterwards.*

Some rules for communicating skill movie trailers:

- **Zoom in as tight as possible** – avoid long sequences. One day is good. One hour is better. Keep it concise. Like a movie clip, it's got to convey a lot in a short space of time.

- **Use slow motion** – reveal the action as it happens by thinking about what you did and how you did it.
- **Use a good screenplay** – does this scene convey a message about skills, about overcoming obstacles?
- **Keep the star in shot** – make sure this scene is about the hero: you.
- **Make sure the clip has a happy ending** – an achievement or a skill revelation.

After five or six skill movie trailers, you'll start to notice a pattern of skills, or a set of *master skills,* and you'll get a strong sense of what you are really good at *and* enjoy doing. This approach also shows you how to communicate skills as concise stories (see Chapter 15).

Further help to identify your skills and achievements

Exercise 6.2 helps you build a list of motivated skills. If you want to cross-check this list or find better phrases to describe your skills, try the **JLA Skill Cards**. This card sort gives you an opportunity to identify your top 10 motivated skills and linked achievement evidence. The cards allow you to choose from a comprehensive and up-to-date range of skills valued in today's workplace. Currently in its fifth edition, this card sort is popular with both job hunters and coaches.

The cards come with a full set of instructions (in booklet and video form) and tips on using skills evidence for your CV and job interviews.

Check out www.johnleescareers.com or search for 'JLA Skill Cards' on **Amazon.co.uk**.

Book readers can obtain a 20 per cent discount on UK orders – email **info@johnleescareers.com** and quote the discount code 'HTG24'.

Sarah, working in engineering innovation

'Like many during the pandemic, I was made redundant. For a long time I had been wanting a career change but wasn't sure how to go about it. I knew I had experience and qualifications but I also knew I lacked confidence.

Looking back, my CV at the time listed everything I did in my job but did not illustrate my achievements. When I started writing my achievements instead, something in me changed. I grew more and more confident in what I had accomplished and how my career experience could be transferred easily to other organisations.

When you lack confidence it's not easy identifying things to promote yourself with. The JLA Skill Cards offered dozens of different skills and all I had to do was choose which skills applied to me. The cards were a catalyst to me seeing I had much to offer an employer.

Career coaching made a real impact when I came to apply for new roles. I stopped looking at job adverts thinking, 'No I can't. . . ', and instead starting thinking, 'Yes I can. . . '. I strongly believe those who read my CV and cover letters saw this confidence – the first job I applied for, I got! I had moved from operations and manufacturing to financial management of research and innovation in engineering.'

chapter 7

Build on your knowledge

'One need not be a chamber – to be haunted –

One need not be a House –

The Brain – has Corridors surpassing

Material Place –'

Emily Dickinson (1863)

This chapter helps you to

- tap your hidden knowledge;
- understand how your preferred interests provide huge clues about career satisfaction;
- focus on subjects that fascinate you;
- make new connections between what you know and work roles;
- explore if 'follow your passion' is the best path.

What do you choose to know about?

Knowledge is poured into us at different life stages. It starts in school, and continues for as long as we receive an education. You read, learn and memorise information to pass examinations, and sometimes to know things useful later in life. When you start work, you learn things because someone else tells us they're important, they will get you promoted or because they enable you to perform the job well.

In school you studied a range of academic subjects, and from the age of 14 or so were asked to make choices about them – sometimes because you have a natural affinity for the subject, often because of career advice about the 'best' qualifications to hold. Inside and outside work, you find some subject areas more stimulating than others. You may have learned things that match your interests and outlook, or things you just happen to find fascinating.

From the first time you borrowed or bought a book on a subject that you couldn't leave alone, you know that hunger to find out more. When you have had the freedom to choose, what have you chosen to learn about? What have *you* decided to absorb? This doesn't necessarily mean formal courses of study. We're talking about those topics you love to read, hear, think and talk about.

Don't just think about what you know, but *why* you know it. The subjects we are attracted to in our own time provide huge clues about the things we want to put at the centre of life, the topics, ideas, people, technologies that make things just a bit more interesting or exciting.

Perhaps there are new areas of knowledge you have yet to discover? Work may open those doors to learning. There will almost certainly also be things you know about that you think have no relevance to work – areas of study that don't appear anywhere on your CV. Or should they?

Exercise 7.1
House of knowledge

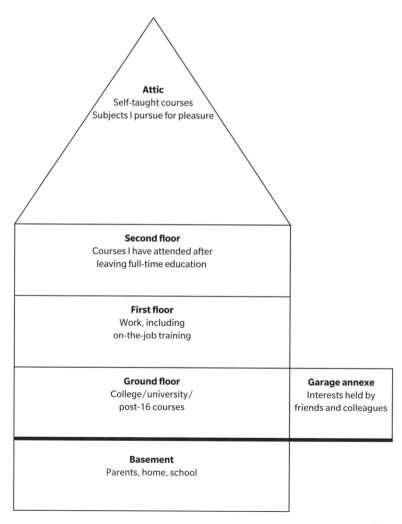

Attic
Self-taught courses
Subjects I pursue for pleasure

Second floor
Courses I have attended after
leaving full-time education

First floor
Work, including
on-the-job training

Ground floor
College/university/
post-16 courses

Garage annexe
Interests held by
friends and colleagues

Basement
Parents, home, school

This exercise helps you identify the things you know about. It will help you record interests that may provide links to potential work sectors. What you choose to learn about is a vital part of who you are.

What do you know about? In answering that question, people usually talk about expertise they use at work, or what they have studied. This is merely scratching the surface.

Look at the multi-storey house of knowledge. It has three floors, an attic, a basement and a garage at the side. Each part of the house represents a life stage where you acquired knowledge.

Like most exercises in this book, this works better if you have a conversation with someone while you are doing the exercise, or as soon as you have completed it.

1   Begin with the **basement** of your house, the firm foundations provided by your home and school. The following questions will help:

- What did you learn from your parents?
- What were your favourite subjects at school?
- What projects or activities engaged you outside the classroom?
- What was the first thing you wanted to read when you put aside your textbooks? What was that about?
- When were you so enthusiastic about a subject at school or college that you went off and found more to read in your own time?

2   Complete the list for the **ground, first** and **second floors**. Think of knowledge areas which do not yet appear in your CV – including the things you forgot you know about. Here are some prompts:

- What training courses have you attended which you found stimulating? Think about (a) courses you chose to put yourself in and (b) courses you were sent on that turned out to be more interesting than expected. What was the topic?
- What subjects led you to turning points in your life (that night school in Photoshop that made you change degree course, for example)?

- What subjects have you enjoyed training other people in?
- What topics have you fallen across in work that you were keen to know more about?
- What parts of your job are you most likely to talk about positively after working hours?

3 Now think about your leisure activities and interests. This is your **attic**, the part of your brain where you store all that old junk you've forgotten you have, stuff you never thought you would find a use for. What areas of knowledge are hidden in those dusty trunks? Some prompts again:

- When have you learned something because *you* chose to do so out of interest?
- When do you find yourself reading, talking or thinking about a subject and others have to shut you up? When do you find yourself so engrossed in an article or a book that the time passes unnoticed?
- Given a free choice, what subjects would you choose to talk about over a relaxed meal?
- Think of a time when you have enjoyed learning about someone else's favourite subject or hobby. What was the subject?
- Which internet pages do you have bookmarked at home?
- If you could teach a workshop on any subject in the world, to any audience and given unlimited preparation time, what would that subject be?
- If you could learn about any subject in the world, from any teacher, what would that subject be?
- If you were accidentally locked into a large bookshop for the weekend, in which section would you camp out? Once you got bored, where would you go next? And next? Write down the headings displayed on the bookshelves.
- Imagine you've received a bequest from an aged relative that will fund a return to full-time education (any subject you like, practical as well as academic, but you have to choose today). What would you choose to study?

- If you won the lottery and didn't have to work, you might spend a year or two indulging yourself, but eventually you would get bored. What might you want to learn about to fill the time?
- What project is literally in your attic, or under the stairs, or stored away in some part of your home?

4 Look also at the **garage**. It's on the side of the house because it represents other people's strong interests. My friend Peter Maybank has a long-held interest in the First World War. I've joined him on battlefield trips to both Verdun and the Somme, revealing what experiences can be shaped by other people's learning.

Look at your complete house. What have you missed out? It'll probably be things you consider 'trivial', such as cooking, homemaking or family history. If you enjoy it, include it. Try to remember all the things you have *chosen to know about*.

- -

Knowledge that won't leave you in peace

The attic of the house of knowledge often reveals more about us than any other part of the building. This is where we store away the special projects, the things that call to us from time to time and just won't go away.

I have had the opportunity to work with some very talented professional photographers. While they're clearing away, I often ask, 'Do you still enjoy photography when you're not doing it for a living?' This is where I discover the themes and projects closest to each photographer's heart. Cheshire-based Richard Weston (Weston Digital Imaging) won an award for a project documenting his son's work as a drag artist. Another photographer, Colin McPherson, gave me a postcard illustrating his long-term work documenting the last salmon net fishermen on the east coast of Scotland.

How to turn your house of knowledge into an action plan

- Show your completed house to a friend. Talk about the activities in your past which filled you with energy. Where is that energy today?
- If you've caught yourself saying, 'I really used to enjoy . . . ', look at why you dropped the activity or interest. How can you pick it up again?
- What can you add to your CV in terms of knowledge?
- What career ideas are prompted by information from any part of the house?
- What ideas are suggested by the subjects in the attic of your house?
- What career ideas are you going to investigate further?

Is preferred knowledge the same as 'passion'?

Chapter 10 discusses how people can feel 'called' to certain kinds of work. The career advice 'follow your passion' suggests that you find your strongest interest and build a career around it.

This idea has its flaws. Benjamin Todd (2014) at 80000hours.org looked at over 60 studies and found that the idea of 'following your passion' can lead you astray. Steve Jobs was a keen follower of Zen Buddhism before entering technology, and Condoleezza Rice was a talented classical musician before studying politics. Todd argues that we can develop a 'passion' for any work that seems enjoyable and meaningful, and job satisfaction involves multiple ingredients: being engaged by varied and stimulating tasks, helping other people, using motivated skills, having supportive colleagues, being treated well by an organisation, having a role that fits your personal life and avoiding major negatives such as job insecurity.

So, if you're thinking that this chapter can be summed up in the well-worn career advice, 'follow your passion', you're wrong. If we feel a strong calling towards a role, it will be partly because we like to think or read about it, but there's a lot more involved – skills, values, impact – just to take three examples. See more on calling and passion in Chapter 10.

Also, a role has many dimensions, motivations change, and we sometimes develop new interests. The idea that a yet-to-be-discovered feeling of passion is the magic key to career satisfaction links to a new absolute – *I have to find my passion before I make a move*. Yet another excuse to think there's no point exploring until the perfect job comes along.

Value your knowledge preferences for what they are, and don't ignore strong interests. They may not map exactly onto your work role, but they provide important clues about potential sectors. For example, if your spare time joy is building boats, you might consider doing this for a living, but you might look at this activity as a set of clues that could point you towards other work areas: for example, working in another craft-related sector, or working in boat sales or supplies, or one of a hundred sectors related to boats and water (see Chapter 9 on identifying sectors). The things you love to know about provide powerful signposts towards work sectors, and your sustained curiosity motivates you to explore them more deeply.

Beth, returning to work after injury

When she began coaching, Beth had been unable to work for three years following an accident at work. Initially, she could see very few work options. She worried about how employers would view her health problems and time off work.

Beth found the tailored exercises her coach offered 'thought-provoking – they really helped me organise what I wanted from a job and from life . . . the end results far outweigh the difficult soul-searching moments. At every stage we celebrated the progress I had made.'

Beth started to look at retraining options with a clearer understanding of the messages she needed to communicate to employers, placing the focus on what she could do rather than on her limitations. She built on her background knowledge and found a permanent role as a practice administrator in specialist practice with an employer 'who values staff and customers equally, but also rewards hard work'.

Beth adds: 'My self-confidence and self-belief have rocketed. When I started career coaching, I was struggling to even contemplate the thought of returning to work and couldn't see how to change this. Then I learned to value what I know about.' More recently Beth has built on something she loves to think and talk about outside work, starting her own online craft business and enjoying the 'freedom of working from home doing something – knowing I've achieved something for myself, by myself!'

chapter 8

Work out your personality fit

'It is absurd to divide people into good and bad. People are either charming or tedious.'

Oscar Wilde (1893)

This chapter helps you to

- see how personality and work are connected;
- celebrate your working style;
- lean towards contexts and roles where your personality fits;
- anticipate psychometric testing;
- understand your values and what happens when you take them to work.

Is personality fixed?

The more we understand about personality, the more there is to learn. There's a good analogy here: genetics. We used to think it was simple to explain how physical characteristics like eye colour are passed on through our genes. Now we know that the answer is, 'It's complicated'. Lots of factors influence the process. The same is true for personality. Yes, you were born with a set of preferences, a default style, but these get tweaked by those big things: culture, upbringing, values, beliefs. We develop an over-arching narrative to express our life story (which can sound positive, neutral or negative based on your picture of what life is supposed to be like).

Science today challenges the view that personality is hard wired. Psychologists argue that we adapt, shift position within a range. Sometimes we do this consciously (for example, an introvert deliberately speaking up in a meeting so their views are taken more seriously) or unconsciously (e.g. instinctively discovering that active listening can improve a sales conversation). We grow and learn, and the more we observe our own behaviours and attitudes, and the more we are able to adapt, the greater the transformation.

Theories of personality, approached thoughtfully, can tell us a great deal about *how* we are at work, and a little about the work contexts we will find congenial, acceptable or difficult. Personality is broadly connected with career choice. If you're a 'people person', you will probably choose an occupation where you work with others, but this could be in a very wide range of work sectors. You may enjoy the socialising potential of work, so won't be too comfortable if you spend a lot of time on your own. Equally, quiet people often prefer their own space where they can plan or reflect without interruption. Even so, introverts can work for organisations which are full of outgoing people. The reality is that a wide range of personality styles can be found in an even wider range of work contexts. Let's focus on *your* areas of comfort and discomfort.

Your personality in the workplace

Work role. If most of the situations you find yourself in match your natural working style, employment feels like a generally positive experience. For example, if you love the opportunity to perform detailed work and that's exactly what you're hired to do. Or if you like seeing a smile on the face of a satisfied customer, you'll probably be happy providing a high-quality service. If you prefer work to be complete and checked, you might find it tricky to work in environments where corners are cut. Where you find yourself outside your comfort zone, your personality and your work may not be a great fit.

Using the right **skills** can be related to personality. Doing things well and enjoying what you do may feed your self-esteem. A mismatch between your motivated skills (see Chapter 6) and your work role can easily make you feel underappreciated.

Your personality provides strong clues about the kind of **team** you would work best in. Look at past team experiences to identify your natural team role: Leader? Diplomat? Progress chaser?

Career drivers (see Chapter 5) have strong links to personality. How many of your strongest drivers match your current role? Look at past roles as well – how does your performance change in a role with a strong match to your hot buttons?

Where your **values** are matched in work, you may feel you're doing something meaningful, and your small part of the world is improved by your actions. Alternatively, if you feel there is something missing, it may be that your role is hollow: productive on the outside, but empty at its core (see Exercise 8.2).

Personality also links strongly with what you hope to find in a **manager**. How do you feel about being micromanaged? How important is it to have a boss who trusts you to get on with the job and supports you even if you make a few mistakes? What opportunities do you enjoy to manage, coach or motivate colleagues?

Do you fit best in a small **organisation** that offers variety and requires self-reliance, or do you need the structure of a large organisation which might offer more opportunities for development? Do you feel constrained by the lack of promotion opportunities in small organisations? Or do you find it hard to be an anonymous cog in a large business?

Working conditions can affect mood and commitment in some personality types. How far is your motivation affected by location, travel distance, what you can see from your office window, where you spend your lunch hour?

Does your job provide opportunities for continuous **learning**? What have you learned in the past 12 months? Who sets your learning agenda? Is your present role a stepping stone to the future? How would a recruiter see your present role: as a dead end, a side alley or a building block in your career?

People seek different kinds of **pace** and **change**. Do you prefer to be constantly facing new problems, or do you need time to deal with the work you're given and to process new ideas? Does change energise you, or do you find it exhausting? Does your organisation make things happen quickly enough for you, or do you feel rushed to submit half-complete work?

Getting a handle on your personality

To start you on an exploration of your personality, think about the following questions:

- What brings you to life? When or where do you become energised? What has a deadening effect on you?

- What kind of people do you prefer to be around? What kind of people do you prefer to avoid?

- What people situations do you find easy? Difficult?

- How far do you need to work on self-awareness, resilience or your emotional intelligence?

- What preparation do you need to answer interview questions about your personality? What are you worried about in terms of personality tests?

- How do you cope with pressure, change and negativity from colleagues?

- What are your values, and what kind of work would match them best?

Exercise 8.1 offers broad indicators about your personality. There are no 'right' answers. Put a score on each scale, avoiding the midpoint. Think about the way you see yourself, the way others see you and the way you react under pressure.

After completing the chart, ask someone who knows you well if you have produced an accurate self-portrait.

Exercise 8.1
Personality overview

- -

Place a tick at the point on each scale which matches the way you see yourself in most work situations.

Confident ———————————————————— Cautious

Head in the clouds ———————————————————— Practical

Abstract ———————————————————— Concrete

Logical ———————————————————— Intuitive

Emotional ———————————————————— Analytical

Optimistic ———————————————————— Pessimistic

Open to change ———————————————————— Reluctant to change

Self-reliant ———————————————————— Need the approval of others

Emotionally vulnerable ———————————————————— Self-assured

Follower ———————————————————— Leader

Solo artist ———————————————————— Team player

Steady ———————————————————— Flexible

What energises you?

People ———————————————————— Solitude

Activity ———————————————————— Calm

Thinking ———————————————————— Doing

Schedules ———————————————————— Improvisation

Groups or teams ———————————————————— One-to-one

Go with the grain

People who seem content and 'level' at work are sometimes described as being 'comfortable in their own skin'. Working with the grain of your personality is often, in the end, better than constantly working against it. Being at ease with your limitations as well as your strengths, knowing your own best working style, not only links to work satisfaction but makes it easier for others to get great value out of you.

Reality TV dealing with career transformation usually encourages participants to 'fake it' – claim skills they don't possess. Genuine selection processes gather information carefully and ask probing questions. Even so, you might still be tempted to project a different personality, or mask elements of the one you have. This is a strange thing to do if you're looking for work that suits you, because it's quite likely to land you a role which feels uncomfortable.

You might worry you aren't intelligent enough for a role. 'Intelligent' usually means 'good at passing examinations', but intelligence has many forms. Some people are good with language, some with numbers, visual images, logic, music; others have highly developed physical skills. Some have few qualifications but practical common sense and problem-solving ability. Some are really good at influencing, others are better at quiet reflection. In other words, people are 'smart' in different kinds of ways.

Watch out for any phrase that begins 'I wish I was more. . . ' or 'I ought to be. . . ', because this really means 'I wish I was somebody else'. Friends might tell you to be 'more assertive', and new behaviours might alter this. Changing behaviours is fine, but underlying preferences – like being quietly modest – are harder to adjust. When you recognise your own 'grain', the easier it is to adapt, decide to be comfortable with the knowledge of where you fit and where you don't. Don't beat yourself up for not being someone else – appreciate, then celebrate, the person you are.

Identify the contexts where you work at your best, and seek them out. Where you are less effective, develop strategies. Enlist people to cover your blind spots. If you're not good at 'reading the room', ask someone who is to give you feedback after a meeting. If you dislike social events, focus on helping someone who looks more uncomfortable than you. If you're not good at checking documents, ask a favour from an avid proof-reader.

Of course, at interview, your aim is to present the best version of you. Not a fake version, but what *you are like on a good day*.

How your personality may be interrogated

You will be aware of personality tests, but in fact the most common measure is an interview when you will face questions about adaptability, attitude to work, attention to detail, working under pressure and how you fit into a team.

Decode job documents and talk to people who understand the industry you're aiming at – find out what kind of personality does well and what characteristics are most highly regarded. Focus on the listed needs of each role, preparing evidence that shows *how* you work, not just what you do. When you offer stories at interview (see Chapter 15), rather than make empty claims like 'I love deadlines', *show* rather than tell – give examples. Rehearse strong mini-narratives that convey useful all-round strengths like flexibility, working with challenging people, having difficult conversations, problem solving, leadership under pressure, and getting things done with thin resources.

Wanting to disguise your personality – or project a new one – assumes that employers have a narrow picture of what they want. No individual is a perfect match, and most people adapt jobs to fit their strengths. Employers are often flexible, recognising that a broad range of people fill roles, and are often more interested in behaviours and adaptability. If the role really is a weak match, you're probably better off knowing this rather than experiencing rejection or getting a job where you'll be a poor fit.

You may hear questions which sound random or off the wall (e.g. 'if you were an animal in the jungle, what animal would you be?'). This kind of question doesn't provide much information to a selector, but it does show if you can think on your feet and maintain a sense of humour. An employer is trying to assess how team members will react to you, and how you will relate to the wider world, including customers; so prepare for any kind of question that reveals your off-duty self.

Personality tests

There are a wide range of tests used in selection. You might encounter tests of numeracy, verbal reasoning, leadership style or skill. In a recruitment process, psychometric tests reveal aspects of personality that might impact on work performance. The Myers–Briggs Type Indicator (MBTI) is used widely in staff development, but its type-based model is now over a century old. The 'big five' approach has featured widely since 1945 (for example, OPQ and 16PF5). This model argues that personality traits sit on a range, and we shuffle our position along this spectrum depending on mood, circumstances, self-awareness and maturity.

If you're invited to take a test, look it up. All reputable tests have websites offering guidance for candidates, including information about what is being tested, how long the test takes and what the results will look like. Many sites offer sample questions so you can get a feel for what the real test will be like. Useful general guidance is published by the British Psychological Society (www.bps.org.uk).

If you are taking the test online, a few tips: Avoid distractions, find a quiet time to take the test at one sitting, working relatively quickly (software will record those answers you changed or spent a long time answering, or if you stopped part way through). Don't overthink your answers (describe how you are most of the time) and be honest. Attempts at fiction are unwise – tests are designed to spot inconsistency and flag answers which feel like something candidates 'ought' to say.

Test providers following best practice will give you feedback on your results, in a report or sometimes in a feedback session with a trained professional. If there are surprises, it's good to explore them with someone who really understands the test. An alternative is to work with a coach or psychologist who can take you through a similar instrument.

Prepare carefully for interview questions directly connected to test results. A skilled interviewer will want to know more about apparent strengths, and also areas for development. An interview will probe areas where there is an apparent mismatch to the role, team or organisation. Have some good examples up your sleeve to establish balance. So, for example, if a test suggests that you're not highly innovative, offer examples of where you have pushed your limits. Often the key strategy is to offer evidence which shows you're capable of adapting to a wide range of circumstances.

Values

The word 'values' is horribly overused today, widely used by organisations who want us to believe how well they behave. For example, most organisations say they value the environment, diversity, their local community and the well-being of the workforce. Values are easy to broadcast, but hard to embed. They are powerful when they change behaviours and how people are treated.

Values are therefore more than slogans – they are principles we live out. They are judged by outcomes, and when actions and words match, we see authenticity. Knowing the difference between value statements and embedded values matters – especially when it comes to choosing an employer. Most organisations say a lot about their values; how far these words translate into concrete actions varies immensely. Some organisations do the exact opposite of what they claim.

Part of your due diligence as a job hunter is to tell the difference between organisations who 'spin' this reputational information, and those that make a reasonable effort to put values into practice.

What were your values when you began your career? How have they changed? Sometimes we judge our work by the way our values are matched. You might be asked to do something you think is dishonest or unfair, such as the customer service manager who is required to make false promises and lie to customers. You might witness behaviours or language you did not admire. Where have your values been affirmed at work, and where have they been questioned, challenged or flattened?

Exercise 8.2
Revealing your values

- -

Step 1 – Values seen in others

People often reveal their values in the way they behave. What behaviours and attitudes do you **dislike**? (Some words to start you thinking: judgemental, intolerant, lazy, arrogant.)

What behaviours and attitudes do you **admire most**? (Some words to start you thinking: modest, honest, self-sacrificing, caring, creative, brave, encouraging, ethical, reliable, consistent.)

Step 2 – Where your values have been challenged

Sometimes we may feel that work is in conflict with our personal values. For example:

- You were asked to do something you didn't believe in.
- You observed behaviours or language that make you feel uncomfortable.
- You were asked to behave in a way that clashes with your personal values.

Think of a **day at work** where you were in a situation which did NOT match your values. Record your answers below.

What happened?
Why did the event challenge your values?
Based on this event, how would you describe your values?

Step 3 – Organisational values

Think about organisations you know well, including ones you have worked for. What values do you admire most in these organisations?

Interpreting results

You can use this information in a number of ways. You can look for shared values in a team you might be joining, and you can investigate those organisations and sectors where your values might be matched.

Ruth, charity leader

After more than ten years as the leader of a grant-making charity, Ruth felt like it would be a good time to move on and find a new challenge. She adds: 'I was lacking in confidence, and the roles I was thinking of applying for didn't seem an exact match with the skills I had developed in my current role. This meant that I felt stuck and nervous about taking the next step.'

Career coaching helped Ruth identify her skills and achievements, 'including those that I had been struggling to identify myself. After such a long time in one role I needed help to see what I had to offer a new organisation and to develop the confidence to present that in a compelling way. I also feel I know more about my working style and personality, so I know where I will be a good fit.'

Ruth feels positive about the next stage in her career transition: 'I have not yet made the move, but I am much further along in my journey of identifying the right role and having the confidence to identify my transferable skills and to talk about my strengths to future employers.'

chapter 9

Choose your world

'There is no such thing on earth as an uninteresting subject; the only thing that can exist is an uninterested person.'

G. K. Chesterton (1905)

> This chapter helps you to
> - understand sectors;
> - discover kinds of work you know nothing about at present;
> - map out work sectors you would like to research;
> - understand what gets in the way of investigation;
> - use lateral thinking to help you to identify areas to explore.

Choices

Think of every person who has walked on this planet in its history. Just over 8 billion people live on it today. According to some calculations, one in ten humans who have ever lived is alive right now (world population has never been this big, and we're living longer). This 10 per cent slice of humanity has more choices available to it than any previous generation. Your great-grandparents probably had no more than a dozen obvious jobs to choose from. Today, there are tens of thousands of occupations available. However, we're still using the same decision-making brain as every previous generation.

Putting experience into compartments

When a kindly uncle asks his six-year-old niece, 'What do you want to do when you grow up?', he's expecting to hear a job title. We're conditioned to think that way, from early age, knowing almost nothing about work. Later in life, in social situations, you're asked, 'What do you do?' – someone looking for the same label.

Society likes to put ideas into boxes. This begins at school. You didn't have classes called *Thinking*, *Speaking*, *Imagination* or *Wisdom* (you might have done if we still followed Renaissance ideas about education). In the Victorian age, educators reclassified what was taught into narrower boxes (and at the same time invented new subjects, including English and Physics).

The problem is that these classroom subjects *seem* to point towards career paths. This 'educational funnelling' limits early thinking. We encourage young people to choose around four subjects at A-level and then one subject at university. This might set up a false expectation that job choices are also being narrowed down. However, few degree subjects *directly* relate to the jobs graduates perform.

Connections between study subjects and occupational choice are often weak. If you're good at languages, you'll think about translation, teaching or possibly working in export/import. Beyond that you may run out of ideas. If you're good at music, art or drama, well-meaning relatives will remind you that creative artists struggle to make a living, and 'you can always do it as a hobby'. Options close down; soon you're drifting towards 'sensible' jobs. If you're good with numbers, written or spoken communication or computer applications, choices broaden. School subjects rarely have a direct link to sectors – there are few people practising 'pure' geography, history or mathematics in the world, and there are many top-level generalists. How do you know where you might fit into the world of work?

Sectors – and choosing them more carefully

One way of thinking about all the jobs in the world is to sort them into groups. Imagine an office block full of filing cabinets. Every job in the world, from aardvark handler to zebra painter, has its own file. You might want to group similar jobs together, perhaps all the jobs in one industry. You might then group industries together. Groups like this are known as 'fields of work' or *sectors*. Some sectors are huge, such as health, education or engineering. Others are smaller, like cyber security or art therapy.

You can find people who seem to be happy whatever sector they work in. Someone who enjoys networking computers, for example, probably doesn't mind doing the job in a factory, hospital or office building. For others, the sector really matters, like an accountant who prefers her work with an environmental charity rather than previous roles in retail. You might be dissatisfied at work because you're in a sector you don't find interesting. Sectors are powerfully attractive when they connect with your strongest interests, your values and with people who see the world the way you do.

Working with products, technologies, brands or people who inspire you can offer a direct link to job satisfaction. People who love their work often say 'it's a great industry'. Once you find a sector that seems intrinsically interesting, curiosity drives you forward and enthusiastic questions come easily.

Think about what enlivens you, and what dampens your spirits. If you don't think your work makes a difference, and you don't have anything interesting to say about it after working hours, there's a chance that a change of sector might be what you need.

Resources for investigation

How do we discover sectors, and find out what it's like to work in them? In the past we relied on careers libraries; today key information is a mouse click away. Investigate sectors using comprehensive sites (start with prospects.ac.uk). Look at TV programmes about work (e.g. Barak Obama's 2023 Netflix series *Working: What We Do All Day*). Research organisations within sectors, noting the titles of jobs you see mentioned. Check out online video interviews where people talk about their jobs (e.g. careersbox.co.uk). You can also find out about organisation cultures and job satisfaction levels through websites such as glassdoor.com. If you're thinking about retraining, look at a wide range of options, some free of charge (see The 'Retraining Directory' at careershifters.org under the 'Learning & Inspiration' tab).

Problems you will encounter when choosing sectors

Problem 1: Not knowing what's out there

Choosing from unknown careers is like planning a journey using a road atlas full of blank pages. Sector discovery is about making maps. Discover the way sectors are changing fast, and look for new ideas, new organisations, new approaches and technologies.

If you can't find a sector that suits you, then look for a new angle. Work is changing so rapidly that new sectors are being created all the time. Before Galileo, there wasn't a discipline you could describe as experimental physics. The word 'scientist' wasn't invented until the 1830s. Before Freud, there wasn't a sector called psychoanalysis. The world wide web was made available to the public in 1991, but took several years to become established, and now has thousands of jobs connected to it. The internet has transformed the way we work, and yet it's still a new phenomenon, being revolutionised by AI. Something that has transformed society has only been around, in human terms, for a heartbeat.

Problem 2: Second-hand information

A huge amount we know about sectors is coloured by the (often half-informed) opinions of family, colleagues and friends. When people describe jobs, they attach value tags (safe/risky, dull/exciting, boring/cutting edge, routine/varied). Sometimes this information points to a truth. Far more often the advice is out of date, based on false assumptions, or just wrong.

You might be tempted to find a career test listing 'suitable' jobs. These interest inventories don't look at the full mix – your experience, values and motivated skills. Additionally, tests that generate job titles have no hope of keeping up with the wide range of jobs available, or revealing how jobs with the same title vary. Tests can usefully point towards sector ideas – they should suggest, never dictate.

Don't rely on the jaded views of retired professionals, recruiters or friends – find out for yourself. One characteristic about people who have made brave career changes is that they became excited about what they didn't know, and started to fill gaps in their knowledge. Often they didn't believe the first person who said 'it can't be done'.

You begin to know what's out there by being fascinated by what's out there. Active exploration, not endless reflection, is the key to forward movement.

Problem 3: Choosing too narrow a range

It's easy to choose sectors that are established, and miss new, growing or changing sectors. Watch out for a blinkered or sentimental reliance on one sector as the only solution.

Let's say your interest is in forestry. You like working outdoors in the wild woods; forestry seems the perfect sector. Training adds to your knowledge of conservation. Your first job focuses on conservation, but you also deal with peripheral problems such as record keeping, grant applications and car parks. Less and less of the knowledge you value is being tapped, and you are increasingly learning about regulations, funding and government initiatives: possible career crisis. You find yourself saying, 'I came into forestry because I want to be close to nature, but I've become a bureaucrat.'

I hear the same story almost every week from people in teaching, HR, nursing, travel, university lecturing and ministry. What I hear is this: 'I was attracted by nursing, and I liked what it said on the label: caring for people, being there for patients and relatives. I got promoted. What do I do most of the time now? Paperwork and meetings.'

Problem 4: Exploring from a distance

Exploring sectors can look like desk research. Yes, you'll uncover basic information this way, but you won't understand how it fits together, or *what the work feels like.*

Trawl for basic information online, then notice what questions arise. Instead of clicking from one website to another, find someone to talk to. Arrange for your first springboard conversation (see Chapter 13) with someone easy to approach. Remember the great question to ask about any job: *What do you do most of the time?*

This process is about *decoding,* not just information. When people talk about their roles, you learn how to translate your skills. And if information and decoding weren't powerful enough, face-to-face conversations have another impact: *visibility.* Asking great questions and showing genuine interest in a sector means you'll be remembered – sometimes in a way that brings you closer to 'hidden' jobs (see Chapter 12).

Problem 5: How do I know if I'll like it?

This question gives away a dangerous assumption: *the only way to find out is to take the job.* Taking a job to discover if you like it is one of the nation's favourite career strategies. You might do this because it's the first job to come along. You might take it because of promises made at interview, or advice from friends that it would look good on your CV.

No one should take a job without knowing enough about the role, organisation and sector to be fairly sure that the role is a good match. Not a perfect match – 70 per cent is healthy (see Chapter 3, and Chapter 15 for ways of interrogating a job offer). Doing background research on the real requirements of a role makes you a strong candidate, but also shows whether it will suit you.

The question, 'How do I know if I'll like it?', reveals something about confidence. Did you notice a moment of hesitation before you wrote down the name of a sector you want to explore? Good old 'yes, but' is at play again: *I'll never get into this sector. I don't have the training. No one will take me seriously.* Don't let assumptions slow you down. This stage of exploration isn't about you, but what's *out there.* Investigation will show you how far you match role requirements. When the time comes to win someone over at interview, you'll know how to manage your evidence.

Problem 6: Moving on from subjects to sectors to choices

Career changers often get stuck. They identify subject areas that look fascinating, but they can't make a connection between a subject of interest (for example, history) and work sectors. They succumb too quickly to 'either/or' thinking (see Chapter 1): sectors are *either* for work *or* pleasure. Friends suggest you 'follow this interest in your spare time'. Most of us work such long hours that spare time interests are often put on the back burner for several years.

This relates to another job myth: *If you turn a hobby into a living, you will fall out of love with it.* This mantra comes from an era when people had plenty of spare time after work for interests. In today's 24/7 economy, it's more common to find people who work, shop, do their laundry, sleep and get back to work.

This work myth ignores the fact that some people say, 'I really love what I do, and I can't believe someone's paying me to do it.' Working with causes, ideas or people that motivate you means that work is energising and feels like a valuable part of life. 'Hobby vs work' is another bit of binary thinking that stops you thinking beyond the obvious. Sometimes (especially if you're going through a midlife realignment) it's important to find things that feed the tired soul.

Problem 7: I can't find anything inspiring

If nothing excites you, it could be because you're too exhausted by work or other pressures to find quality time for career exploration. If so, take some time out to recharge your batteries, and find encouraging friends to keep your spirits up (read about support teams in Chapter 11).

You might be applying unhelpful filters (probably encouraged by others). You might have dismissed sector ideas because 'they won't pay enough', because 'I'll never get an interview' or they're just plain wacky. Often you have to move well outside safe territory to find something that floats your boat. Explore as if you were doing it for someone else – no filters, no early decision making in the wrong place – just gather ideas and build on them.

Problem 8: I want to choose something quickly

The ability to seek alternative options is a thinking tool easily pushed to one side. The mind has a natural longing for certainty. A training colleague had a phrase for this: 'Don't confuse me with facts, my mind is made up.' Don't worry if your sector ideas seem random or disconnected; the world of work is fluid. Test ideas, group them together, keep focusing on the next step.

You may come up with what you describe as 'too many' sector ideas – a potential recipe for indecision. Move on from brainstorming (generating as many ideas as possible), to prioritising – create a short list to stop reflecting and start acting. Decide on no more than six sectors for detailed exploration. Don't make a final choice between them yet – just explore. Wherever possible, turn an idea into a question and a question into a conversation.

If you can't see how you can move from subjects to potential sectors, you need to join the dots differently. Look back at your house of knowledge in Chapter 7. What subjects fascinate you? What do you love learning about? What work activities are you eager to talk about at weekends?

Exercises in this chapter point you to sectors. Make sure these *are* sectors – 'consultancy' isn't a sector, but a way of working; 'management' is a function. Are your sectors too big? Look at subsectors. For example, if your sector is marketing, ask yourself what products or services you want to promote. What names are given to these subsectors and jobs inside them? Picking up the language helps to open more doors.

115

Switching sectors: The challenge

Do you want to change what you do or the sector you work in? Look at the options, and the increasing levels of difficulty:

1 It is straightforward to remain in the same occupation, but switch sector – for example, remain an accountant but switch from manufacturing to transport.

2 It is (relatively) straightforward to find a new occupation without changing sector. For example, you may remain in insurance but move from being a payroll administrator to become a learning and development specialist.

3 It's harder (but certainly not impossible) to change occupation *and* sector at the same time. You will need even more detailed research – find people who have already made the move. Perhaps consider a stepping-stone approach: change one element now, and another in 12 months' time, when you have gained relevant experience.

From discovery to action

Reimagining career possibilities gives you places to look. The key next stage is *finding out*. This book provides all kinds of prompts to activity, so let's nail down one plain fact. If you want to put off career change forever (or at least until it's too late), then keep on reflecting, analysing and mulling over. Keep on thinking that you have to make the perfect decision before you act. That will happily prevent change. If you don't want to spend your last inactive years saying 'I wish', do *something* – and do it soon.

Finding out – following your enthusiasm – costs very little. You don't need to have a perfect target job to start the process of discovery, just a sense of curiosity. And here's a big clue: Your breakthrough probably has a tiny chance of happening as a result of reading or thinking, and a huge chance of occurring as a result of *other people.* Someone you already know really well, possibly. Or someone you choose to *get to know* – someone you meet in the next three months as a result of your enquiries.

So, what's the first step? Obviously, a conversation. Start with someone easy to approach, even if they have no obvious connection to the sectors you want to explore. Find opportunities to talk to people who seem to love what they do for a living.

---

10 steps towards deeper sector exploration

1 Look back at your working life. Identify sectors you have found satisfying or interesting. Why?

2 Think of people you know who are doing interesting jobs. What's interesting about them?

3 What jobs have you seen advertised that caught your attention for 30 seconds, even if you did nothing about them?

4 Talk to people in interesting jobs. Find out how they got them.

5 Draw up a list of sectors that interest you. Set out a plan for investigation.

6 Arrange springboard conversations (see Chapter 13).

7 Become a future watcher. Read articles about how sectors are changing.

8 Tell people about the sectors and ideas you find exciting, asking where you could explore further.

9 Investigate career ideas thoroughly – as if you were researching for somebody else.

10 Use the ideas grid (Chapter 16) to list target sectors and prompt further exploration.

Exercise 9.1
Sector match

- -

Subjects that interest me	Obvious matching sectors	Not so obvious sectors	Wild ideas	Example organisations
Creative writing	Copywriting, journalism	Internal communications	Lobbying	

1 In column 1, list subjects that interest you. Use the house of knowledge (Chapter 7) to help identify them. Add any extras that come to mind.

2 Against each subject, record at least two **obvious matching sectors** – for example, if you have put 'history' in column 1, obvious sectors for column 2 might include *museums, conservation*.

3 Now think of two or more **not so obvious sectors**, asking yourself, 'Where else are people who know about this subject employed?' (e.g. *documentary making*). Do your homework (e.g. Google 'Career ideas for language learners').

4 Add any **wild ideas** that come to mind. Don't dismiss anything; be as imaginative as possible.

5 Ask friends for suggestions in all columns.

6 Research interesting new sector ideas suggested.

7 As you think of names of example organisations, list them in the right-hand column. Use these example organisations as targets for your contact list (see Exercise 13.1 – The connections game).

- -

Exercise 9.2
Combining work ideas

- -

1 Work on your list of sectors that interest you until you have 10–15 sectors. Write them out on cards or Post-it notes.

2 Redefine any phrases that are too broad (e.g. 'Management', 'Consultancy').

3 Divide your cards into two piles – first choice and second choice. Your first-choice pile represents sectors you will prioritise in your investigations.

4 Pick six sector cards from your first-choice list which particularly appeal to you. Put three in a row, and then three in a column, as below. Put a piece of paper between them and draw a nine-square grid in the empty space.

	Card 1 Physical fitness	**Card 2** Languages/ translation	**Card 3** Export/import
Card 4 Creative writing			
Card 5 Health & safety			
Card 6 Ecotourism			

5 Try to come up with a sector or subsector to write in each blank square. A completed example is shown below.

	Card 1 Physical fitness	**Card 2** Languages/ translation	**Card 3** Export/import
Card 4 Creative writing	Writing creative self-help books promoting fitness	Translating novels	Writing export guides
Card 5 Health & safety	Safety awareness in personal fitness regimes	Translation of specialised safety management texts	Exporting products and systems relating to safety management
Card 6 Ecotourism	Carbon-neutral sports events	Translating commercial tourism ideas into ecotourism	Importing ecotourism practices from another culture

6 Use these new sector ideas to prompt investigation (find out about entry routes, qualifications and training required, measures for success, prospects).

- -

Melissa, operations manager, third sector

After leaving university Melissa felt lost, not knowing what direction to take. She tried the health sector for a while then discovered she enjoyed working with children with special educational needs: 'I loved going into school every day and working with the children. However, I did not want to study for a teaching qualification, and wanted more responsibility than being a teaching assistant. I took a career break abroad for two years – this was perhaps an attempt to escape the real world of work and finding my career! When I returned to the UK I felt more lost career wise than ever!'

Melissa writes: 'My coach encouraged me to talk to people rather than sit trawling through internet job sites. I felt demoralised by rejection, but created a CV focused on communicating what I really wanted from a job. By networking my way to an agency, I landed a role as a support worker focused on autism. After two months I was promoted to management. I had found a job where I was giving something back but it also gave me the responsibility that I had craved.'

'I have since moved on to other exciting roles in the third sector, building on the confidence I gained from my first big career change'.

chapter 10

Changing career and finding work worth doing

'Pressed into service means pressed out of shape.'

Robert Frost (1914b)

This chapter helps you to

- rethink the idea of 'career change';
- begin with small steps;
- look at the way we choose career paths;
- consider finding work that feels more purposeful, or more like a calling.

Career change

Let's tackle this 'change of career' idea, which is how we describe a change of sector. Some argue that we have just one career built from multiple experiences – relationships, learning, work and everything else that engages or distracts us outside work. Incidentally, you will do better at interview if you talk about a single career story rather than apologising for 'changing career' or 'switching paths' or any other loaded language which implies that (a) there's only one, conventional way of having a career, (b) any progress you've made is entirely accidental and (c) you have no idea where you're going next.

So how do you begin if you want to add more colour, more variety to your single, integrated career path? Perhaps by looking for a new role, new sector, or both – finding new challenges, perhaps learning new things. This might already be on your radar, and it might not look easy.

Changing career is more demanding than changing jobs. It's a journey into the unfamiliar that will require new information, new ways of thinking, unconventional behaviours and other people to inform and support. Deciding to change career increases risk: small risks of rejection, and big risks that it will all go wrong. For some, this has to be managed while holding down a job. So, learning how to achieve small things without burning your boats is important.

Small steps

The media reinforces the idea that deep down we all have a dream job. Some stories suggest that you might find it in 24 hours. Newspapers love stories of 'accountant becomes skydiver' or 'commando becomes nanny', reinforcing the idea that just having a positive attitude can make this happen overnight.

Rapid movement like this is relatively rare. People progress by gradual steps; they 'try on' careers experimentally (read Herminia Ibarra (2003) to learn more about incremental career changes). Many do this in their first ten years of work when it's relatively easy to change direction and experiment; but others do it later in life, developing a 'side hustle' or building a portfolio career.

Jim Bright has a great take on career decisions. In his book with Robert Pryor (2011), he applies chaos theory to careers work. He suggests that random events play an important part in career choice; we rationalise decisions in hindsight, but most are improvised responses to an unpredictable world. Bright found that about three-quarters of people have changed direction because of an unplanned event, and argues the value of seeking out new experiences rather than trying to plan and predict (see shift projects in Chapter 3).

'Career change' often means moving to a new sector, or a major change of lifestyle. Either can seem risky (as people will take delight in reminding you) because this is about moving from known to unknown. It helps to begin with subjects that fascinate you. If you want breakthrough, take small, exploratory steps. Commit time to exploring sectors of interest, keep an open mind, try ideas on for size, and keep looking.

How do we choose a career?

In a first session with a client, I ask about past, present and future. 'What has motivated you in the past, both within work and outside it? What was the best job? The best organisation? What's going on right now that makes change attractive?' Then we move to 'What next?' Clients often say they have no idea what they'd like to do next, but they usually know something. I think it was a US careers specialist who stated that everyone in the world knows exactly what they should be doing. The problem, he said, is that half haven't found the words to describe what they're looking for. The other half know exactly what they should be doing, but are too frightened to say it.

As Chapter 9 argues, we are funnelled into sectors of work by academic choices. However, many influences shape career choice.

People and other influences in career choice

- **Parental norms** – occupational groups tend to repeat themselves in families.
- **Parental expectations** – young people are encouraged towards careers that match what parents believe to be the right kind of work.
- **Academic subjects** – what you choose to study may seem like the key to your future.
- **Money and status** – academic high achievers are often pushed towards high-pay, high-status occupations such as law, finance or medicine.
- **Peer pressure** – doing something cool; avoiding things that look boring.
- **Advice from your first boss** – the opinion of your first manager often shapes the way you plan your career.
- **Personal values and beliefs** – the kind of work that seems worthwhile.
- **Media influence** – the jobs we see done on TV or in films or online.

- **Teachers and lecturers** – pointing you towards the roles they know about.
- **High visibility** – jobs you see around you all the time.
- **Careers advisers** – particularly influential while you are also making study choices.
- **Work-related tests** – ranging from bona fide personality or interest inventories to something you found on the internet.
- **Personal inclination** – your strong (or vague) sense of what might work, what you are 'supposed' to be doing or what you feel called to in life.

The first item above – parental norms – is more influential than you might think. We gravitate towards jobs that touch our lives, jobs we see happening. When children spend a lot of time in hospital, they often want to be a nurse or a doctor. There's a useful modern slogan used to encourage diversity: *if you can see it you can be it*. In a TV programme about a remote Indian Ocean island that lacked even a school or post office, a young boy was asked what he wanted to do when he grew up. 'Fishing', he said, naming the one job he could see available to adult males.

Work on screen

Even in our developed society, we are exposed to only a fraction of the jobs available. For example, do you know what a gamification marketing specialist does, or a diversity guru or a metaverse storyteller (three job titles that didn't exist five years ago)? New types of jobs are created every day.

Some jobs are much more visible than others. You know what a surgeon, a barrister or a firefighter does. More accurately, you *think* you know, but how much of your perception is based on what you see on TV? Some jobs are never off the screen (medics, lawyers, teachers, police officers, CSIs, chefs), others shown rarely (when did you see an offshore rigger, 3D designer, personal shopper, car valeter, or order picker?). Some occupations in the same sector are given very different weighting: TV loves architects but tends to ignore surveyors.

There is a reason for this. Television features jobs that work visually. It's more interesting to show a crime suspect repairing a car than photocopying, more interesting to set a conversation in a flower shop than an office. This shows us a limited and distorted picture of work. When you see a police officer in a crime drama or documentary, you see someone chasing and apprehending a criminal. Talk to actual police officers and you discover that even those on the 'beat' spend most of their time doing one thing: responding to emails. TV prefers the more exciting moments: the airline pilot avoiding a crash, the lawyer bringing in a surprise witness, the medic diagnosing a mystery illness.

What would you do if. . .

The great benefit of 'what if. . . ' questions is they allow you to put the dangerous word 'realistic' aside for a moment. Ask yourself, 'What if I could do *anything*?'

You might have been asked, 'What would you do if you won the lottery?' People who have won millions in lotteries may surprise you in their choices. After playing with the money for a year or two, buying houses, holidays and cars, they tend to get bored and look for occupational activity – yes, some form of work. Since money is no longer a reason to work, they look for purpose. This might mean investing in a business or starting a charitable foundation, or it might be taking up a simple trade. One lottery winner went back to his job as a staff trainer for McDonald's restaurants. So, if you win the lottery, what will you do two years later when you're bored? What seems like *purposeful work* to you?

Exercise 10.1
Purposeful work

- -

Stage 1: Remembering

- Jobs you imagined doing in your childhood. What sectors (see Chapter 9) do they suggest?

- What are the most enjoyable subjects you've studied? How might they relate to work ideas?

- Where have you been in work which felt purposeful. Why?

- Jobs done by friends or family which you find fascinating.

- What jobs have you seen advertised in the past which attracted you (even if you never applied for them). What about it was attractive?

Stage 2: Three great days at work

- Think about a time when you had a great day at work. The sort of day where everything went well and you went home energised. Write down what you were doing, what you enjoyed and what you achieved.

- Do the same thing for another two memorable days.

Stage 3: Imagining

- What jobs have you ever imagined doing?

- If you could try someone else's job for a day, what would it be?

- If you could do any job in the world for a week and still receive your normal salary, what jobs would you try?

- Who are your role models or champions, and what sectors are they in?

Stage 4: Trying ideas on

- What jobs have you tried, even for a few hours or days?

- What job on your CV was the most stimulating?

- What would you like to try next?

- Who could you interview or work shadow to find out more?

- -

Career change: Just do it

Reimagining career possibilities is engaging and useful, but when you discover an idea, the key question is, *what are you going to do about it?* If you want to put off career change forever – keep on reflecting and analysing. Keep thinking that you have to find the one perfect idea before you act. That will happily prevent change. If you don't want to spend your last inactive years saying 'I wish', do something – soon, especially if you have a sense that some new kind of work will feel more authentic, purposeful, more *you*.

Many years ago I heard a motivational speaker in San Francisco deliver a great one-liner. I've tried to find the speaker's name, without success, but I thank him anyway. He said: *If you only live half your life, the other half will haunt you forever.*

Deciding what or who?

To answer the question, 'What kind of work would suit me best?', it helps to think about the unique mix of experience, knowledge, personality strengths and values that you have to offer. Let's look at three overlapping areas – what you are, what you do and what you know.

Three career circles

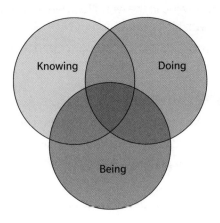

Knowing

Chapter 7 revealed how preferred kinds of knowledge provide powerful clues about meaningful work. Think about *what you have chosen to know about*. What topics, interests, ideas matter most to you? What topics do you like to talk and think about? Where can you find them (or something like them) in the world of work?

Understanding how knowledge fits into work might also make you think about each job as a learning curve. Most roles are interesting in their first few weeks or months, but whether a job is interesting in the long run is often about whether the results you achieve are intrinsically interesting, and how much you have opportunities to learn and grow.

Doing

The phrase 'You are what you repeatedly do' has been misattributed to Aristotle, but it's a strong idea. What we do shapes us, particularly actions we repeat every day. You can turn this around: What we *choose to do* most of the time matters. The activities that take up most of our waking hours have a strong influence on our effectiveness, work outcomes and the way people see us, and also on whether we feel our life makes a difference. Remember that word 'occupation'? A job is something that 'occupies' time and attention.

Skills (see Chapter 6) are what we repeatedly do. They move us towards outcomes, they shape our reputation and they are important reinforcers of self-esteem. They can be absorbing, fascinating, motivating. Your favourite skills may need to be refreshed and sharpened, but first of all they *need to be used*. Using only part of your skill set, or using skills you don't care about, can lead to long-term demotivation and cynicism.

Being

How you exercise skills reflects who you are – your working style, motivation, personality and values. To perform a task well, accurately, with care, considering the needs of other people, and to be positive-minded or resourceful under pressure – these are not only signs that you have an attitude to work which keeps you feeling engaged, but also an indication that you've found work that seems worth your attention.

'Being' links to personality. You're born with certain traits (see Chapter 8), then acquire attitudes and principles as you age, but also values. When we talk about values we're describing behaviours and principles that matter. Where someone's values are aligned at work, that often means the work is meaningful. This is highly individual; what seems like dull work to one person can be satisfying and meaningful to another.

Consider the kinds of work that allow you to 'be yourself', or work that feels more like a 'calling' (see below). Look at outcomes – what does your work create or make happen? Does your work improve the world, make someone else's life better, build or create something worth sharing? When it comes to work, *being* and *purpose* are intertwined.

What's calling you?

Do you sense that deep down you're not looking for a job, but for a *vocation*? The word comes from the Latin *vocare*, 'to call'. It's used most frequently in terms of a life of faith, but even in popular usage a 'vocation' feels different from an occupation. Not only have we redefined what we mean by 'career' in the past 50 years, we have redefined what we mean by 'vocation', too. Some feel a 'calling' towards working with animals, being a chef, creating fine art photographs, making handmade furniture, working as a civil servant or serving in the armed forces. Perhaps what these paths have in common is the connection to a big idea or cause, often the knowledge that your work enhances the public good – people are helped, taught or lifted up by your daily work.

Sometimes a calling is connected to a love of materials – a photographer appreciating the quality of a lens, an artist enjoying handmade paper, a cabinet maker absorbed in the wood and the tools as well as the urge to make something beautiful. You might feel enriched by the words and ideas you have the opportunity to share. You might feel inspired by the connection you make with people whose lives you touch or change.

When we feel 'called' to the work we do, this provides a sense of commitment stronger than ordinary motivation, and a sense of 'rightness' in our choice. It's not just a career impulse, not just this year's big idea. Feeling 'called' can provide a strong sense of 'right fit' – you've found the place which is authentically *you*. Rowan Williams (1995) wrote: 'Vocation is . . . what's left when all the games have stopped.' A calling may be about finding the best version of yourself.

Following this path might result from faith or strongly held personal values. Whether it's about doing something with great care or serving needs, vocations make an important contribution to society. A vocation may draw on particular gifts, or awaken abilities you didn't know you had. Other callings are simple acts of dedication.

Does a calling make you happy?

A vocation often means turning your back on conventional career satisfiers such as money and status, and it is a pathway that may take years. It feels more accurate to talk about 'following' a vocation than choosing it. As Magdalen Smith (2019) writes, 'Vocation is often an unknown journey which involves humility as well as courage.' Many vocations require a commitment of decades, some a whole life.

You may therefore assume that a calling means forgetting about work satisfaction: it's a matter of duty, not personal contentment. This is an unhelpful starting point. There will certainly be a sense of purpose, and often some sacrifice, but living out a vocation can be deeply fulfilling, and might lead to a sense of contentment that is deeper than surface-level happiness. Many people talk about their calling as a joyful privilege. This positive experience isn't the same as 'fun', but shouldn't be a million miles from it. Work that is a calling should enliven you, at least some of the time. There are, however, many glum-looking people in teaching, nursing, church ministry and charity jobs. Your vocation may be useful to society, but if it makes you miserable, you may be performing the wrong role in the right cause.

Perfection is often a dangerous idea, especially around calling. Those living out vocations will admit that they are not 100 per cent committed to their calling all of the time. The difference is they keep faithfully to the path, honouring that original calling, living out long-term life choices even when things are difficult. Perhaps the key feature of a vocation is this: *it's not just about you.* So, three tests that might help. In a vocation:

1 The role feels right for you and others can see it's a good match for your gifts.

2 You commit to a long game, which may include fallow years.

3 You offer something which helps, feeds or inspires other people. A vocation is a life lived for others.

Even if you don't feel you have a calling in the big sense of the word, something of the above might help you find purposeful work. Remember that what you learn about finding it and learn about yourself on the way may help others on the same path. Share what's worked for you, warn others about bear traps and dead ends. If you learn how to find purposeful work, *pass it on.*

Exercise 10.2
Paths not taken

- -

Consider important turning points in your life – moments when you had to choose a path. Record a number of key turning points as below.

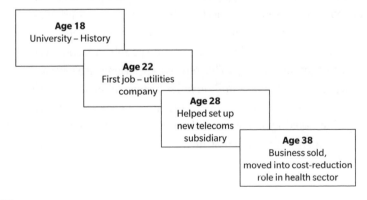

Age 18
University – History

Age 22
First job – utilities company

Age 28
Helped set up new telecoms subsidiary

Age 38
Business sold, moved into cost-reduction role in health sector

Look at **one** of your turning points. Write it in a box in the middle of a piece of paper. Then draw out your **paths not taken as below.** **These are the alternative choices which were on offer at the time** – things you nearly did or could have done. Your final diagram might look like the following example.

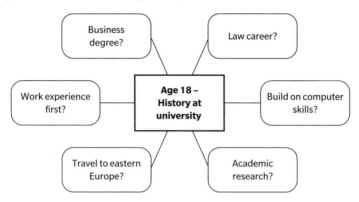

Questions about your paths not taken:

- What choices were available to you at past turning points?
- How did you choose each path?
- What difference would a change of path have made to you?
- What does this exercise tell you about the way you make career choices?
- What paths feel as if they are calling you next?

- -

Will Beale – Head, Network Standards, WWF

Having studied natural sciences and chemical engineering, Will worked for Unilever for a decade before looking for work that matched his values: 'I spent three months undertaking information interviews with about 40 people in my target sectors. I learned a lot, but uncertainty about the future meant it was also quite a tough time, especially for my family.'

➤

Will applied for a wide range of jobs – business, NGOs, public sector. His dream to work for an organisation focused on environmental sustainability and nature conservation turned into a real opportunity at WWF. A few months into the new role, Will emailed John Lees: 'Almost unbelievably, I am here in Rwanda with gorillas in the mist.'

Will has been with WWF for 20 years and is now on the staff of WWF International, with oversight of WWF's management and quality standards. 'What I love most is the chance to work with a project in detail – for example, helping a team or organisation to develop a great strategy, or evaluating the impact of a major programme.'

He enjoys the challenge of persuading the general public to think of WWF as being about more than wildlife protection: 'We focus strongly on underlying issues such as climate change and unsustainable consumption.'

chapter 11

Dealing with knockbacks, and getting stuck

'The voyage of the best ship is a zigzag line of a hundred tacks.'

Ralph Waldo Emerson (1840)

This chapter helps you to

- cope with the predictable highs and lows of job change;
- plan to deal with rejection;
- get to grips with the word 'realistic';
- get 'unstuck' if you feel you're not making progress.

Following the cycle

Looking for a new role can be emotionally demanding – trying to make a career change even more so. Put an ordinary person into job hunting mode, and they behave differently to the relatively self-assured person they were just a few weeks before. Typically, job hunters say, 'I'm comfortable reaching out to new people when talking about my organisation – but not doing it for myself.' Presenting *you* feels risky, because when someone says 'no' to you – to *your* life experience, *your* abilities – that feels personal. Even confident people start to show signs of uncertainty the first time they get a knockback.

Most of us, in transition, become vulnerable. You face the risk of rejection every day, often in isolation. Every setback can impact the way you see yourself, how you see everything around you and can easily change behaviours. That's why this chapter deals with the cycle of affirmation and rejection.

Even if you've only applied for one or two roles this year, you know about the ups and downs of job hunting. You get up days when you're invited to interview, when someone returns a call requesting an information interview, when someone reminds you of something you did well. On these days, naturally, you feel more confident about your abilities, sometimes capable of doing anything.

You will probably have down days as well. This might happen if you don't get shortlisted for an obvious role, or if you get pushback from a recruitment consultant. Often the main reason you're feeling dejected is silence. You've applied or reached out, and heard nothing at all. You might be feeling low because a friendly contact hasn't returned your call, or just because it's raining.

If this rings true, you're someone who is affected by criticism or rejection and more prone to negative self-talk. Even expected or minor knockbacks might slow you down. You start to overprocess, beat yourself up. If you don't monitor these low moments carefully, they influence choices and behaviour. This is the point clients email me to announce they have no transferable skills, or they've applied for a boring job they really don't want.

Recognise what being at the low point in the cycle feels like, then promise yourself not to make an important decision at that moment. Don't redraft your CV, send an important message to a high-level contact, finalise a job application and *don't* make a career decision. Do something that lifts your spirits – run up a hill, watch a movie, schedule a meeting of your support team (see below). The up point will come, and that's the moment to pick up the phone or try something new.

The high/low game

Career changers of all generations, but especially market entrants, operate in high/low mode. Fresh graduates apply to high-profile employers forgetting that these organisations are swamped with applications. Having failed to get onto the shortlist for one or two 'five-star' jobs, they aim lower – much lower. They apply for low-profile, less interesting roles because they look easier to get. They apply for jobs which could be done by someone with far less experience or qualifications. They begin to talk themselves into taking whatever comes along.

This can mean taking a role that adds little to your CV and gives you problems in years to come. You're unlikely to get shortlisted for attractive roles in well-known organisations, especially if you apply cold without knowing what buttons to press. But if you can't persuade doors to open for five-star opportunities, dig deeper to find out how you can get closer to four-star roles.

Even if you don't get the job, you can learn a huge amount about your perceived market value. It's trite to say that you shouldn't feel rejected if turned down by an employer. It may take a while to bounce back, and that's both understandable and predictable.

Rejection, data and noise

In an average job search, you will be rejected more times than accepted. This neutral statistic has nothing to do with you or your CV. You will hear 'no' more often than you hear 'yes'. Even the best salespeople in the world know they need to hear the word 'no' at least three times before they get a 'yes'. The problem is that when the 'no' is to your experience and abilities, it hurts and can knock you off balance.

All this happens very easily. You hear the word 'no' a few times, and use it as evidence. You come out with new absolute statements: 'I knew my background wasn't strong enough. . . '. You start rewriting your CV and talk about lowering your expectations.

If you're shooting wild, applying for everything, every rejection is random. You might assume a whole set of reasons why you don't get an interview, but recruitment processes are much more arbitrary than you know. Often a huge volume of applications are received and your chances of being noticed are slim. Sometimes the employer rethinks the job, or imposes an unexpected hiring freeze, or has always planned to give it to an internal candidate.

As you reach out, learn to be more objective about results. The most common response from the market is radio silence. Busy people sometimes need to be nudged politely several times before they respond. Many employers don't send any kind of reply to job applicants. If you hear nothing back, you have no data, just guesswork. Don't fill the silence with fake information. Collect information, not hunches. If half a dozen seasoned recruitment consultants tell you there are absolute barriers to getting shortlisted, or you discover that a sector is in terminal decline, that's hard data. Everything else is just random noise.

Being cautious about 'realistic' thinking does *not* mean that your next move should be made without any reference to the real world of employers and hiring decisions. That's what informed exploration is all about – discovering what's real and out there, really understanding role and sectors and how to get closer to them. Pushing negatives to one side is a key part of the process.

Stop looking for negative reinforcement

There are more varieties of jobs out there than ever before, yet many accept second-best because it's easier to stand still than to move forward. We sometimes like to do what feels safe, even if that means being unhappy. There's a powerful part of the brain that says: *Stop here. It's dull, but it's comfortable. Out there looks difficult and strange.* Next, you seek out evidence to support this. You find stories of people your age and background who tried to make a change and failed.

I have a theory. Because we are vulnerable during change, we go into self-protection mode. We switch on a personal radar that scans the horizon for information. Radar, as you know, is hungry for enemy objects. And we find them. You discover people who were made redundant and never found a job again. You find that people beat a path to your door to tell you, 'Don't do it . . . it will all come to tears.' Half-consciously, you look for 'evidence' that allows you to stay immobile.

You'll find all kinds of limiting statements to block growth and change. If you keep saying, 'I'm not an ideas person' or 'I'm useless with IT', soon you believe it. Once you believe it, it becomes a self-fulfilling prophecy. If a golfer says, 'I bet I slice this ball', she probably will.

I'm indebted to Marie Brett, who told a story at one of my masterclasses for career coaches. She overheard two women on a bus in Northumberland talking about a daughter who was trying to find a job. 'These days', one explained, 'it's not about what you *want* to do, it's about what you *can* do.' Marie could hear the poor daughter's career derailed in one sentence. Another coach, Esi Kpeglo, talked about trying to reposition herself midlife, building on her professional background. An elderly relative suggested, with real kindness, that it might be time to find a 'humbler' job like being a pot washer or postal worker. Other people shape our career thinking, and can easily reinforce negative assumptions.

Being 'realistic'

Remember that word that came up in Chapter 3? It's still around, nipping at your ankles as you try to step forward. *Realistic*.

Listen in to everyday career conversations. Two friends have met for coffee, and one is talking about job options. Her friend asks, 'What are you looking for?' The answer begins: 'Well, in an ideal world . . .'. For a short moment there is a touch of excitement. Then, half way through the sentence, something changes in tone: 'but, to be realistic. . .'.

The word 'but' is a pivot point, between positive energy and downbeat acceptance. Between an interesting 'ideal' world where work might be fun, and a less exciting compromise that often feels like trading down. Whether voiced or not, one word hangs over the conversation. The word *realistic* – as we've seen, the most dangerous word in the career changer's vocabulary.

So-called 'realistic' thinking can stop you at the first hurdle. Under pressure, choices simplify. Stay or go. Fight or flight. Stress makes us reach for either/or thinking – turning a multicoloured world into black and white. So, as with the overheard coffee shop discussion, you might find yourself using one of the nation's favourite polarised statements: *Either I find a job I really enjoy doing, or (to be more realistic), I find a job that pays the bills.* That sentence sounds like an internal debate, but it isn't. The decision has already been made. You're going for 'realistic'.

The word *realistic* slows you down, because it is rarely about what is *real*. The word masquerades as something objective. It pretends to be fact-laden, researched, but it's usually about fear of the unknown. 'Realistic' advice is often second-hand information, someone else's picture of the world, often based on how work was 30 years ago. If you are told to be 'realistic', ask yourself: *Whose reality*? Listen to the people who are telling you to 'lower your sights'. What does that say about their own life experience and mindset? What does it say about their unlived lives?

It really pays to spend time with positive-minded people. Optimism provides energy, and energy matters if you want to change career – you'll need it to sustain you, and you'll need it when you communicate your skills to potential employers.

Exercise 11.1
Getting unstuck

- -

This exercise helps you go back to an earlier stage in the process of change, and review where you are now. Write down your answers in the blank boxes.

1. What prompted you to start reading this book?	What's changed?
2. What were the most important things you wanted to change?	Are they the same now?

➤

3. What choices did you want to see when you started to think seriously about your career?	What choices do you see now?
4. What has worked well for you since you began some of the activities suggested by this book?	What has worked less well?
5. How do you feel about your current situation?	What happens if nothing changes?
6. What one action might make the biggest difference for you now?	Who can you find to encourage you to take this step?

Look at the six pairs of questions. Be clear about problem areas, but also look at where you have made progress. You might find the question, 'What happens if nothing changes?', is powerful. It might remind you of the real impact of work dissatisfaction, or what will happen to your well-being if you keep banging your head against the same brick wall forever.

- -

Working smarter rather than harder at career building

Some say the perfect job is out there looking for you, but you can't stay home and wait for it to drag you out of bed. Most of us have to rely on a mix of active investigation, supportive contacts and luck. Luck has been described as two mathematical laws working together: chance and averaging. We can't control chance, but we can increase the odds in our favour. Invest in your future. Work at creating and building on ideas; a moment's inspiration can sometimes take you much further than a year's dull planning.

Setting objectives is a vital part of the process. Ideas without activity are just ideas. You don't need to wait for a brilliant career idea, a lucky breakthrough or great contacts (although any of the last three will shorten the process). What you do need is to plan to take one step, soon, and then take the step after that. That's how change happens.

Information is neutral. It's easy to put all your attention on things you believe you lack. For example, 'I can't . . . ', 'I've never been good at . . . ' and so on. Self-limiting statements do what they threaten to do – limit your choices. They're often completely arbitrary and unfounded, but easy to adopt as your new reality.

Think broadly. Exploring is about the wider view, the deeper perspective. We tend to think along tramlines, moving logically from one stage to the next. Divergent thinking works rather differently. Let your imagination fan out: rather than making decisions too soon, look at possibilities.

Exercise 11.2
Career transition diamonds

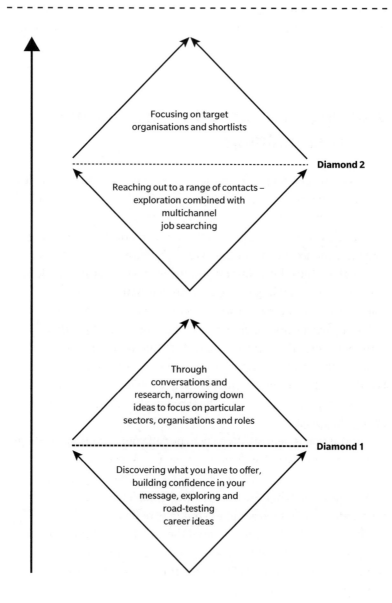

Focusing on target
organisations and shortlists

Diamond 2

Reaching out to a range of contacts –
exploration combined with
multichannel
job searching

Through
conversations and
research, narrowing down
ideas to focus on particular
sectors, organisations and roles

Diamond 1

Discovering what you have to offer,
building confidence in your
message, exploring and
road-testing
career ideas

Look at the **career transition diamonds**. Where are you in this process?

Diamond 1 represents the first phase of career transition. This stage is about experimentation and idea building, but it's not about introspection. Turning ideas around in your head is far less effective than testing them out in real contexts. Experiments need a laboratory, and your best laboratory bench is the world of conversations. So even the bottom part of the lower diamond involves action – reaching out to other people to find things out, or try things out.

Open-minded experimentation during this first phase requires a promise. Promise yourself not to find early reasons to say 'no' to ideas. Gathering information means you can choose what to explore in more detail, crossing the dotted line into the upper half of Diamond 1. Decide on a small number of sectors to investigate (see Chapter 9 to help you choose).

Notice that **Diamond 1** has a thicker dotted line across the centre. This represents a danger point where many get stuck. Learning about ourselves can be fascinating and affirming, and sometimes we want to stay in that comforting space. If you find yourself looking for more career exercises, enjoying the inner journey but reluctant to pick up the phone even to the friendliest contact, you might be stuck at this invisible barrier.

The way forward is to remember that each step should involve *doing* something – an activity focused on what's out there. As Richard Alderson points out in his shift projects model on page 36, reflecting needs to lead to acting, from day one and at each stage in the process. Keep learning more about your strengths and preferences, but reach out to understand how they connect to work. So, right now might be the moment to pick up the phone and arrange your first information interview (see Chapter 13).

Diamond 1, the investigation stage, requires you to step outside your comfort zone to discover things. **Diamond 2** moves you decisively into new kinds of action – approaching organisations, following leads, influencing decision makers, moving towards job offers. Diamond 2 is action focused but still requires you to think imaginatively about how you can find new people to help you open doors. To get to **Diamond 2**, you need to make some hard decisions. What sectors? What organisations are you going to focus on? How can you present your best self to get shortlisted? At the top end of Diamond 2 everything has a simple benchmark – *does what I am doing get me closer to a job offer?*

Seeing where to plant your next footstep

Almost everyone trying to change career or look for a job in difficult times gets stuck in the process at some point. These are some of the things that they say:

'This isn't working for me.'

'I'm not making the progress I expected.'

'It's all a bit idealised – I just need a job.'

'I just don't have the energy any more.'

'I'd rather just apply online like everyone else.'

'I've done some networking but I can't find anyone else to talk to.'

'I can't get excited about any of the roles and sectors I've been looking at.'

'I apply for jobs but don't hear anything further, and I don't get any feedback.'

'I feel a bit of a failure.'

'I am thinking of resetting my sights. . . .'

'Nothing is working.'

Look at that final phrase. When coaching clients get stuck, they use absolute language to apply the handbrake. It's a form of catastrophising – either/or thinking on speed. Once you've decided that no strategy is effective, it's easy to want to throw aside everything that's motivated your interest so far. This is a dangerous instinct if you feel stuck.

Two strategies from positive psychology help here. The first is to **focus on what's working**. Trainee commercial airline pilots are taught how to think in an emergency. If an engine fails, they are trained not to focus just on that one component. Instead, they ask, 'What do I have left working which will put my passengers safely on the ground?' In the same way, we can learn to shift our attention away from things that aren't working and decide to place it on the things that are. What strategies are still available to you? What one thing can you try next? If you stay focused on what seems to be failing, you waste energy on conversations that haven't worked and applications that fell at the first hurdle. Everyone gets knockbacks. If you are the kind of person who takes rejection personally, don't beat yourself up about it – recruit some support (see below).

The second strategy is to **do one thing differently**. This is particularly effective with exploratory conversations, and very powerful when it comes to interview preparation. It's based on the idea that many businesses succeed because of the 10 per cent principle. They are 10 per cent quicker, 10 per cent more efficient or 10 per cent cheaper than their competitors. So rather than trying to change everything about reimagining your career, just do one thing differently every day. For example, next time you reach out to someone don't say you looking for a job, just say 'I'm exploring'. And in the same conversation, at the end make sure you say something like, 'That piece of information really resonates with me – who could I talk to next to find out more?'

Recruit a support team

Critics have argued that Jane Austen portrayed two kinds of individuals in her books: people who live and *people who see themselves living*. Self-awareness makes a difference. People who make conscious decisions about their working lives are likely to be more successful and more satisfied. They have thought about the work that they want to do and are actively pursuing it. Some have moved into new roles, and others have redesigned or renegotiated the jobs that they do.

Few things are achievable without the right tools and the right people, especially self-awareness. Yet too many job seekers tough it out alone. Get support.

First, have experimental 'what if?' conversations with people who might give you a different perspective (but make sure the feedback encourages exploration rather than closing it down). Second – and do this before you finish this book – build a support team.

Find **two people** who will meet you and provide help. One person will do, at a push, but a coach–client relationship often happens. When a trio meets (in person is best), you get two perspectives and double the encouragement. The conversation doesn't need to be just about you – help each other in turn. You'll often find that a discussion over a cup of coffee or a bottle of wine works very nicely. The other two don't need to be experts, but they do need to be curious about people, jobs and the world of work.

Recruit the two members of your trio carefully. They should be people who can

- support you in the ups and downs of career transition;

- give you honest, objective advice about your skills, and help you to see the evidence you use to back them up;

- provide ideas for exploration and connections with other people who can help;

- use positive thinking to help you build on your ideas;

- keep you accountable to your plans.

Warning: if you hear a friend say, 'Yes, but, in the real world . . .', or 'It's not that simple . . . ' or 'that won't work', don't invite them to be part of this process. There are thousands of people out there who will pour cold water on your ideas. Choose people who will give you encouraging feedback and positive support.

Alex, graphic designer

Working on the university newspaper revealed in Alex a talent for design. So after graduating she found a job as a designer working for an engineering company. When the recession hit, she was made redundant, and everyone advised her that there were no jobs in design. Her family put pressure on her to look for a 'sensible' job.

She considered alternative career paths, even though they were far less interesting. By exploring her motivated skills, Alex found she 'really was drawn to creative work, but I also had people and analytical skills'. When asked what she would do if all jobs paid the same, it was clear that Alex wanted to remain in the design world.

So, having reestablished what was at the centre of her target, Alex decided to abandon passive strategies. She reached out directly to organisations and people.

Alex explains how the hidden job market opened up: 'I learned not to look for advertised jobs, but to find people who are doing interesting things and may need help.' By making direct approaches to organisations who were not advertising, and demonstrating both skill and enthusiasm, Alex received two job offers within a fortnight of this change of strategy, quickly gaining experience of both in-house and freelance work as an illustrator.

chapter 12

Smarter job searching and online activity

'Attempt the end, and never
stand to doubt; Nothing's so hard but
search will find it out.'

Robert Herrick (1648)

This chapter helps you to

- understand how organisations make hiring decisions;
- discover the hidden job market;
- develop an effective online strategy;
- build productive relationships with recruitment consultants.

If deadlines are tight, read Chapter 14 for a 4-hour job search programme. However, if you want to gain a bigger understanding of how to job hunt in today's market, read on.

How employers prefer to find new staff

Here's some information that on its own probably justifies the cover price of this book.

UK government research has analysed the way employers fill vacancies. The Employer Perspectives Survey (Department for Education, 2017) consulted employers about how they recruit: 81 per cent of employers used 'multiple methods of recruitment'. Some of these involve cost – using recruitment consultancies, for example, or paid-for job advertisements. Other channels cost little – Jobcentre advertising, job postings on the organisation's own website or social media pages.

One method is entirely free and stands out in terms of popularity: 79 per cent of employers surveyed used word of mouth or personal recommendation. Smaller establishments and new businesses said they rely heavily on this method. It seems to be on the increase; nearly three in ten employers surveyed *only* recruit this way.

This slightly old-fashioned phrase 'word of mouth' refers to an informal connection between someone who works at the organisation and someone outside it. This could be a telephone tip-off to a corporate executive, someone emailing vacancy details to a friend or someone chatting at the school gate.

The dominating power of social media has changed so much about the way we exchange information. 'Word of mouth' blurs with other channels. For example, a friend may see a Tweet mentioning a hiring need and mention it to you over coffee. You might reach out to the organisation via LinkedIn, make a speculative phone call or go through a formal recruitment process. You might phone a friend who you know is looking for a role like this. Informal and formal, electronic and human – pathways overlap, but invisible connections feature extensively.

Employer safety habits

Building on what we know about employer recruitment methods, it's clear that employers and job seekers use totally opposite strategies, and see risk very differently. We will look at each employer strategy in detail below.

How employers and candidates see risk differently

Perceived risk level for candidates	Employer method of attracting candidates to a vacancy	Perceived risk level for employers
High	1. Personal connections 2. Word-of-mouth recommendations	**Low**
Medium	3. Using external recruiters 4. Finding people using social media 5. Unsolicited approaches from candidates	**Medium**
Low	6. Advertising the job on the company website 7. Advertising the job externally	**High**

Staff are found through personal connections

Organisations know that a low-cost option, and sometimes the best way of avoiding risk, is to hire people they already know. The most obvious example is someone who already works at the organisation. If an employer can't find talent internally, they turn to people who are closely connected. This will include previous employees – these 'boomerang' hires often prove successful. Often senior executives talk directly to contacts who might be potential candidates.

You might feel this is unfair, more about 'old school tie' networks than suitability for the job, but it's still a fact of life; employers prefer people they know something about to complete strangers. 'People we know' doesn't just mean high-level contacts – it could be someone who was an intern or on a work placement recently, or someone conducting an information interview.

Employers act on word-of-mouth recommendations

If an employer can't find someone within their circle of contacts, they ask around for recommendations – because that's almost as good as 'people we know' and costs nothing.

You might be recommended through someone who has known you for a long time, or someone you met recently in an information interview. You might be known because several people in a sector have mentioned your name. It's all about visibility.

Look around you. Who admires what you do and would be happy to recommend you? Have you enlisted help from these people as mentors, career coaches, dummy interviewers, idea factories?

External recruiters

Many organisations work with recruitment consultancies. This is relatively expensive (the employer normally pays a percentage of starting salary), but agencies are good at filtering applications and attracting talent. The employer gets to review a shortlist of people without having to advertise, screen random applications or send rejection emails.

For the job hunter, recruitment agencies are important intermediaries between you and employers with jobs to fill. They are gatekeepers, deciding who to put forward. Their role is to fill the job, but they can provide objective views on what you're communicating and how you interview. Many have extensive market knowledge. Working with external recruiters has positive and negative aspects for job hunters (see later in this chapter).

Social media

If an organisation can't find staff through personal networks, it might reach out via social media. This is free and can draw in individuals who have been following the organisation online.

Social media can therefore alert you to vacancies and employer needs. Reaching out to useful contacts through LinkedIn (see later in this chapter) can also work well in terms of setting up information interviews.

If you respond to a vacancy via LinkedIn, ensure your profile is up to date and lists relevant skills, sector information, organisation names or technical details to attract the attention of an external recruiter (see below for LinkedIn tips).

Unsolicited approaches from candidates

Unsolicited applications (speculative approaches where there is no apparent vacancy) can get bad press – from candidates who email untailored CVs on a 'spray and pray' basis and get no reply, and from organisations who receive them.

Where an employer has announced that a vacancy exists, direct expressions of interest are welcomed. Speculative approaches open doors more often than you might think, but need to be highly targeted, matching organisational requirements (or more general industry needs). Organisations are interested to hear from you if you can solve a problem or build on an opportunity. Approaches like this work best if you can get an introduction rather than relying on a cold email.

Organisational websites and social media pages

An organisation putting a vacancy on its own website is speaking to multiple audiences – current staff, those following the organisation online and people directed towards roles through tip-offs and recommendations. Apply with careful attention to detail, matching your evidence against job requirements. Research the role through your wider network, and stick carefully to the rules of each recruitment process.

External recruitment advertising

When a role is advertised, employer risk increases. The floodgates now open. Job advertisements are known in the recruitment industry as *candidate magnets*, and many applications are off target. Even if you offer relevant skills, your chances of being shortlisted are low – just because of the volume of traffic – yet many people put most of their time into chasing advertised roles.

Don't exclude them from the mix, but don't rely on them. If you apply, get noticed. In your covering email, set out half a dozen bullet points of evidence which match key job requirements. Someone relatively junior may be shortlisting, probably into three piles: 'No', 'Possible' and 'Yes'. In a competitive market, the 'Possible' tray is dispensed with. Work hard to get that initial 'Yes' to move forward to interview.

The hidden job market

Having looked at employer recruitment preferences, you may be coming to a conclusion: Chasing conventionally advertised jobs, particularly online, may not be the best use of your time.

If you want to slow down your job search, limit your search to advertised positions. You'll miss out on most newly created jobs and many jobs in small businesses. You'll miss out on all those companies thinking about creating a new job. You'll avoid opportunities where you are recommended – or doors opening because you've asked great questions.

Studies show that about a third of jobs internationally are filled through word of mouth. Similarly, about a third of job seekers find jobs this way. This relates to *all* jobs, from shop floor upwards. With highly skilled, professional or niche roles, the proportion of jobs filled through informal contact increases significantly. In many sectors, senior or specialised roles are never advertised. The hidden job market seems mysterious, the stuff of urban legend, because so much goes on under the radar. Most know that the hidden market exists; few know how to break into it.

What's running through your head right now? *You're going to tell me the answer is networking.* Well, in a way – your way. Find out more about organised discovery in Chapter 13.

'Open' may still be 'hidden'

You might feel strongly that the 'fair' way of job hunting is to apply only where a role is openly advertised. If so, be warned. 'Unhidden' jobs, for example those advertised in the third sector, may not be as 'open' as they look. An internal candidate may already be lined up, promised the job a long time back. At other times employers have a preferred candidate but want to 'benchmark' by looking at outsiders. Advertised positions can also have a 'hidden' flavour: You might be told that a job is about to be advertised and encouraged to apply (therefore automatically shortlisted). This happens even in the public and charity sectors.

Jobs are filled every day without the world having any sense that a vacancy ever existed. This can in fact take a lot of stress out of job hunting. If you meet an organisation and they like you, a job may be created around you. If an employer finds you through a recommendation, you can easily find yourself in a shortlist of one.

Job hunting online

Reaching out or hiding behind screens?

Before mobile phones, job hunters stayed home in case the phone rang. Now we sit at our desks and pray to St Google. Why do so many people believe applying online is the best and only method? First, it's easy – job sites are readily accessible from handheld devices. Second, sitting at a screen uploading your CV *looks and feels like work.*

Some years ago, I helped at a job club near San Francisco. Even in a buoyant, hi-tech economy, jobs weren't all that easy to find. The club had a rule: *Use your PC outside working hours. During the day, use shoe leather.* The web is fantastic for research, reasonably good at making connections, but not always great at opening doors.

It's all about the power of memory. A Tweet can be forgotten in seconds, an email in minutes, a phone call in under an hour. A warm face-to-face meeting can be remembered for over 12 months. Even though online meetings are now the norm, in-person conversations remain the gold standard.

Job boards are best used as part of a multistrategy approach. Register with sites that handle relevant jobs or specialise in interesting sectors. Be aware how applicant tracking software (ATS) screens your CV – research and use relevant key words. Search recruitment sites by specialism, sector, role title or by location. Use them unconventionally, to spot hiring organisations and useful recruitment consultancies. Learn about job titles, and how sought-after skills are described. Don't ignore company social media pages, where you may come across jobs not advertised elsewhere.

Making connections that matter

Relationships matter in a job hunt, especially if you want to change career. Online activity should support relationship building. Your aim is to build an electronic support team: connections who will provide you with ideas, information, encouragement and introductions.

Social media provides new contacts (who update their own details), but think about what these contacts notice about you. Eventually you'll signal your employability, but as you begin exploring you might not know exactly what you're looking for. That's acceptable. Use LinkedIn to mention things you're curious to know more about.

Managing your shop window

Be certain: If your name comes up, people look you up on social media. Can they find you? Having no online presence slows down progress and suggests you have no interest in modern communication tools. If you have a LinkedIn profile which is sketchy or considerably out of date, this signals a lack of care about the way you communicate. You have a shop window, but no one has changed the display for a long time.

For work, LinkedIn is the main marketplace. It's a space used by a lot of recruiters, and key phrases can attract interesting traffic. LinkedIn is widely used, easy to manage and all about working life rather than opinion or pet photographs. Explore the job-seeking options LinkedIn provides, where you can define the type of employer you're looking for and list skills. You can add videos, and longer form content like articles, or point readers to a personal blog. It's designed to enhance visibility, leading to connections with people who don't know you, and recommendations from people who get to know you.

On LinkedIn, you can scroll down to see full content on any page, but the first screen is the one that matters. That's where an early decision is made to read more (just like the first half page of your CV). These are the essentials:

- a **customised URL** (go online to find out how to do this) – short and easy to place in a CV;

- a **photograph** that makes you look professional and easy to get along with;

- a **headline** that captures what you do. This doesn't necessarily have to be a real job title, but something that makes you easy to place, e.g. 'qualified procurement specialist'.

- useful **contact information** – an email address outside LinkedIn is useful;

- a short **profile** – an opening paragraph that sets out your main experience, key skills and what you're interested in right now.

After that, request a few **recommendations** – ask people to write about what you have done, not just your personality. Then populate the rest of your LinkedIn space: work history, education, qualifications, awards – but remember these are normally checked when someone has already seen something interesting in your profile. Ask a friend to summarise what they read on that first screen. How would someone know what you do, immediately? Are you including useful key words in your headline, summary and work experience sections, so people and software can find you?

LinkedIn offers free or low-cost job advertising for employers. Recruitment consultants use it to find candidates, so check your message box as well as incoming emails. Recruiters are always working against the clock and will often work with the candidates they can reach quickest.

LinkedIn is a relatively serious business space; be mindful of your online reputation. Ensure that on-screen coverage of your wild side is visible only to trusted friends. Employers and recruiters use the internet for background checking. If you post photographs of yourself in a state of undress or inebriation, you might as well bring them with you to the job interview – it's called *public domain* for a reason.

Search LinkedIn using organisation names – click on 'Follow' for news about people and organisations you want to keep in your sights. Join the largest relevant groups – participate, contribute and reach out to users. Search using job titles to find people in interesting roles; ask mutual acquaintances for introductions.

Relying exclusively on LinkedIn is a workable strategy, but Twitter can also be useful for spotting industry and company news and vacancy announcements. Also, many key influencers use it as a platform. This can provide big hints about organisational culture – executives are likely to be more conversational and less guarded on Twitter than in other outlets. Tweet interesting links and occasionally ask questions. Avoid expressing strong opinions and getting involved in online spats, because this will also be revealed if someone looks you up.

Using social media when you're between jobs

LinkedIn offers special graphics to show that you're open to work, but it's better to talk about your experience, not your availability, so it's not always a good idea to talk about being unemployed. Phrases like 'looking for next great opportunity!' sound like mild desperation. You may, however, get away with a clear, focused and unemotional statement, such as 'seeking full-time employment as an HR Manager in the East Midlands area'.

Make sure your online profile shows you're active, not just waiting for the market to come to you. Refresh material with updates on the things you are researching, for example: 'Reading everything I can get my hands on about healthcare reform . . . ', or 'Just watching a fascinating presentation on green building construction'. Show that you're up to date; put in live links to websites, blogs, videos and podcasts so that readers can learn more about the things that have inspired you. Bookmark interesting pages so you can recommend links on a drip-feed basis rather than all on one day.

Reaching out through screens

Focus on an organisation that interests you. Follow key players online, then consider an approach. An email out of the blue is likely to be ignored, so ask yourself: 'What can I do to avoid sending a cold email?' Ask around, or use LinkedIn to spot people who work in (or used to work in) your target organisation. Put out an email to 20 friends asking if anyone knows anything at all about an organisation or has a useful contact. If someone mentions a name, pick up the phone and ask for an introduction – this is quicker and more effective than messaging through LinkedIn.

Working more productively with recruitment consultants

Recruitment consultancies can play an important part in a multistrategy approach, if you know how to work with them (see Joëlle Warren's advice at the end of this chapter). Be clear about what they do. They are not in the business of providing career advice; they fill jobs for employers by finding suitable candidates. Agencies range from high-street operations to executive search consultancies ('headhunters'). Although recruitment consultants keep candidate databases, they are largely vacancy driven, and most interested if you fit a vacancy that needs filling quickly.

Recruitment consultants have a huge advantage compared to you as an individual: they have leverage to persuade an employer to commit to interview dates and issue job offers. When you have a fairly clear idea of roles you're aiming at, establish contact with about 12–15 agencies who frequently fill relevant positions. You will be asked to register online, but try to establish a relationship as well. If you spot a suitable role, find the name of the consultant handling it and ring up with a detailed or technical question only the consultant can answer. Recruitment consultants like to be valued for their industry knowledge, and often agree to talk to you if they can learn something about the organisations you've worked in.

External recruiters can offer objective feedback about your CV and interview technique, tell you what you are worth in the marketplace and what hurdles you will have to jump to change sector. Less professional agencies will flatter you on registration and never come back to you. Some don't know as much as they should about a job, and some will be reluctant to put you forward if you haven't done a similar role in the past.

Many recruitment consultants have strong views about CV construction. Don't ask, 'What do you think of my CV?' Ask instead, 'What does my CV say to you?' Listen to the story coming back at you. If you recognise and like what you hear, your CV is working well enough.

Working with executive recruiters

Joëlle Warren, Founding Partner, Warren Partners

The following no-nonsense tips from an executive recruiter show how you establish and build good relationships with recruitment consultancies.

1 Focus on being exceptionally good at your job and making a positive impact. Good headhunters will then find you – but make yourself visible to them so that they can. Writing articles, speaking at conferences and receiving industry awards all help.

2 Identify recruiters who specialise in your industry/function and build a relationship before you're in job search mode by using your network to gain introductions and being helpful and considered when you're asked for recommendations; then prioritise who you want to stay in touch with. Don't forget you are divulging confidential information about yourself and potentially your employer, so do your homework around the recruitment company's reputation, expertise, values and ethics. Do they feel a good match?

3 Strategically target the consultant within a firm who specialises in your function or sector. This individual should facilitate connections to colleagues who might be pertinent to you – but you may need to ask them, particularly if you are open to changing sectors. Recruiters have a habit of putting you in a box, so it's better if you choose the box (or boxes) you want to be in. It is not necessary to contact multiple individuals within the same firm.

4 In terms of cold calling a headhunter, email is still preferable to a phone call as a first introduction due to the heavy volumes headhunters receive, since it gives a quick

impression of you and allows the headhunter to circulate your credentials among their colleagues and enter them into their global databases. The headhunter will immediately look for what is unusual or uniquely differentiating in your CV, so it's important you include quantitative information such as the size of the jobs you have held, organisations for which you have worked, the number of people you have managed and results/profits for which you have been accountable.

5 The email accompanying your CV should give a quick snapshot of your career drivers: title, geography, compensation and the types of opportunities you are interested in. If you do send a cut-and-paste email to a variety of headhunters, make sure it's personalised and all the typeface is in the same size and font!

6 Avoid 'spamming' headhunters with multiple unsolicited emails each week or phoning them several times in a day, as these efforts may backfire.

7 Be transparent without being overly self-promotional during any phone or in-person meeting with a representative from a search firm. Do not make claims that will not stand up to rigorous background and reference checking – the headhunter's duty of care to their clients necessitates a reasonably thorough investigation of candidates, and they will quickly discover anything that is fabricated or exaggerated.

8 Assess opportunities proffered by headhunters realistically. Do not feign interest in a job that you are not intending to follow through on simply to get facetime with a recruiter – it will waste their time and not position you as a serious candidate.

9 When meeting the recruitment consultant, always have in the back of your mind that first impressions count: be prepared, be punctual, be smart, don't be afraid to 'use' the headhunter – ask for honest feedback on interview performance.

10 Once you've had a positive meeting or telephone call, ask the headhunter for their preferred method of staying in touch – phone or email – and how often.

11 Demonstrate that you 'know how the system works' by offering to help with open assignments; enhance your reputation with the headhunter by referring friends and colleagues that you hold in high regard (assuming they're at the right level and in a relevant sector) to them.

12 Be open with the headhunter about which firms you are trying to establish a relationship with – ask if there is anyone they would personally recommend. Share openly and honestly how the rest of your job search is going.

chapter 13

Organised discovery: How people will move you forward

'It requires a very unusual mind to undertake the analysis of the obvious.'

A. N. Whitehead (1925)

This chapter helps you to

- rethink networking;
- develop a two-breath message;
- understand the benefits of information interviews;
- learn how to have springboard conversations.

The difficulty of doing the obvious

If I have a client looking for a new role, I ask them which job search method is most likely to work for them. Even at this stage clients sense they will get better results through people than screens. However, they are reluctant to do anything that looks like networking.

Many people just hate that word, *networking*. They say it feels 'grubby', 'pushy' or 'it exploits people and loses you friends'. Some are even more honest: 'It makes me look desperate.' We should respect these suspicions. Anyone who suggests you start networking without addressing these issues is trying to get you to buy a jacket that doesn't fit, isn't your colour and is something you'll never wear after you take home.

Later, when someone has found a role, I ask: 'If you find yourself looking for a job again, what will you do differently?' The answer is nearly always, 'I would start talking to people earlier.' Not 'networking', you notice, but simply *talking to people*.

There are lots of reasons for talking to people. When an exciting opportunity comes out of the blue, this is rarely a random event. It happens because you have done something to manage your visibility and what other people know about you.

Networking for softies

Networking has acquired a tarnished reputation. You might imagine pushy breakfast meetings where you're supposed to 'work the room', handing out business cards. You might think you need to sell yourself. Both kinds of activity can be as unproductive as they are dispiriting. Be kind to yourself, and network like a true softie.

Don't call it networking. Call it *meeting interesting people* – a way of following your curiosity, not exploiting others. Networking should never be about trashing friendships for the sake of a job offer. Networks are *social* networks – they work best when we take a genuine interest in others, sharing ideas and information – what has been described as a 'chain of helpfulness'. Often you will form lasting relationships of trust.

Think of it as *building a community of interest*. Communities work not because of the total number of people, but the connections between them. If four people are connected, that's 12 relationships. If you simply add one more person to the group, you get 20 relationships. A mailing list may be 2,000 separate, unconnected people. An interest group as small as 2,000 can overturn national policy.

We connect with helpful people all the time. If you move to a new town and need a childminder or plumber, you ask around, without worrying what the request sounds like. Start with practice runs with people who are easy to approach. Take a friend out for coffee and say, 'This may come out all wrong, but can I try this out with you?' Try out questions – about the work people do, how they got into it, the overlaps between their world and yours. Thank contacts for their time, but don't say goodbye until you've asked the number one, all-time, breakthrough question:

'Who else should I be talking to?'

Degrees of connection

Daniel J. Boorstin said, 'The greatest obstacle to discovery is not ignorance – it is the illusion of knowledge.' (Krucoff, 1984). We think we are aware of the limits of what we know.

In 1990 John Guare's play *Six Degrees of Separation* premiered in New York. Its title reflects the idea that you can reach anyone in the world through a short chain of connection. Person A leads you to B, B to C and so on. Even if you begin with only the vaguest connection to your target, you will get there in six conversations – or fewer.

I regularly ask if anyone in an audience has met someone who has been into space. Twice in my life I came close to famous astronauts without even trying (Yuri Gagarin was Manchester's guest of honour while I watched from my pram, and 40 years later Neil Armstrong spoke at a venue ten minutes' walk from my office). The first manned space mission was in April 1961; since then only a few hundred people have been into space. Yet it's not hard to find someone who has talked to an astronaut, and sometimes these conversations are life changing. Even the most extraordinary people are not that far away.

If I'm with a group interested in career change I often invite participants to turn to the nearest stranger and ask one question: *What are you looking for?* If there are 300 people in the room, about half a dozen will sneak out at this point. This is sad – the 140-plus conversations that follow will include some amazing moments. Later someone from the audience will always find me and say, 'You know, I've just had a conversation which may have changed my life.' The fact that it happens every time means *it just happens* – you just need to ask the question.

Information interviews

A job interview is a conversation seeking a job contract. An *information* interview is different: a conversation designed to reveal useful information about a job or a work sector. They have many benefits, but are used by a minority of career changers.

An information interview is the subtlest, easiest form of connecting with people. They are not about selling yourself – mostly not about *you* at all. This isn't pushy networking in disguise, and you're not subversively trying to obtain a job interview.

Information interviews are *really* helpful if you plan to change sector. Why? Because you don't know what you don't know. If you apply for roles, you're guessing at organisational needs. Desk research will help, but you get there much more quickly by talking to people. They give you the inside story – what it really feels like to do the role – as well as insights into organisational culture and industry trends.

It's a low-stress process, because you're armed with a script (see below). Start by finding someone you know well who does work that interests you – someone you can ring without having to plan what you will say.

Information interviews – why they are useful

☑ **Information benefits of information interviews**

- For a critical time, you put *research* before *job search*.

- You meet people in real jobs by moving from desk research to field research. You will learn about entry routes, sector trends and organisational cultures.

- You understand the reality of jobs, so you can begin to decide if they will suit you.

- You spot roles and sectors that match your skills and experience.

- You pick up clues that will help you match yourself to specific roles.

- You understand how top performers are described.

- You pick up skills and language useful in job interviews.

☑ **Visibility benefits of information interviews**

- People remember you, especially if you see them face-to-face and thank them in writing afterwards.

- People remember your energy, your enthusiasm, your commitment, your reason for enquiring.

- The people you meet make connections on your behalf. Your name is mentioned when problems and opportunities arise.

- You learn enough information to sound like a credible candidate really committed to moving into a new sector.

- You are often talking to decision makers, putting yourself on their radar.

- You plant carefully chosen information about you which is remembered.

☑ **Job-seeking benefits of information interviews**

- You learn more about jobs using this method than by applying randomly for roles or asking to be told if a vacancy comes up.

- You identify target organisations.

- When people understand what you're looking for, they can help you. If you're remembered, opportunities find you.

- You pick up insider language that allows you to convince people you really understand the sectors and organisations you're targeting.

- If you broadcast employable skills and knowledge via social media, you may get direct approaches from recruitment consultants.

- Your visibility may put you straight onto a shortlist, even if a job isn't advertised.

- You discover jobs before they become vacancies.

- *You fall over jobs.* It's true. Ironically, the indirect route, which is not focused on job search, often turns out to be the number one strategy for getting at the hidden job market. The roles you discover might not be right for you – if so, pass them to others in your network.

☑ **Confidence benefits of information interviews**

- You learn how to ask great questions and convey memorable energy.

- You get used to talking about yourself without overdelivering or feeling fake.

- You learn how to make your experience and skills sound relevant to new sectors.

- Since you're tracking down people who share your vision of what work is about, you'll end up with new social contacts and friends.

- You (sometimes) get to wear smart business clothes and visit places of work, which maintains your confidence levels in a job search.

- You leave people with a positive impression of you, and enough information to recommend you to others.

Big and small asks

Asking someone for career advice is a 'big ask' – it takes a lot of time to read a CV properly and then give feedback. Information interviews work because they ask for something much smaller. People find it easy to talk about themselves and their role, and if you make the conversation painless, they'll often suggest someone else you can talk to.

Ask for 11 minutes of the person's time. 'Half an hour' is vague. You can conduct a springboard interview (see below) in around 10 or 12 minutes. Asking for 11 minutes gets someone's attention, and shows you're focused. If you stay longer, it will be because you are invited to continue the conversation. Don't ask to be shown round the site, but accept the offer if it is made.

Ask for a face-to-face meeting. You learn far more – about the person and organisation, and you stand more chance of being remembered. Online is second best, but worth taking, especially if a contact is a long distance away, when you might ask, 'Who do you know in my part of the country . . . ?'

Don't use the term 'information interview', just ask for a conversation. It's an interview, yes, but don't make it feel formal or like an interrogation – if people enjoy the experience, they will disclose more. Don't ask too much, don't stay too long.

Springboard conversations

You've got there – you're in the room with someone who can help you. What on earth do you say? Here's a five-step method for conducting information interviews (the example shows a springboard conversation with someone in event management – adapt the script for other roles and sectors).

Landing zone 	*'I'm here because I've been told you really know about event management, and I'd love to find out more about it.'* Mention how this meeting has come about, especially if someone introduced you. Be clear what you hope to get out of the meeting. Possible follow-up statements: *'I'm aiming to talk to a few people to find out more about this industry.' 'I'm really interested in. . . .' 'My questions don't take more than around 15 minutes'.*
Biography zone 	*'Can I start by asking about your background. How did you get into this line of work?'* Asking a little about the biography of the person in front of you breaks the ice, and sometimes tells you about sector moves. Possible follow-up questions: *'What did you do before?' 'How difficult was it for you to move into event management?'*

**Role zone**	*'I'd love to know more about your role here. What do you enjoy most about the job?'* This is the main question, so allow your conversation partner plenty of time to answer. Focus in detail on role content. Ask additional and probing questions so you really understand the role. Listen carefully for the language used to describe different tasks. Summarise to check facts. Follow-up questions: *'What's not so great about the role?' 'What's your biggest challenge?' 'If you could change one thing about your job, what would that be?'*
**Bigger picture zone**	*'That's really interesting. Can we talk now about the event management sector as a whole? What's changed in the last year or so?'* Now you're looking in broad terms at the sector or industry, finding out about current and future trends. Follow-up questions: *'What skills do people need to do well in this sector?' 'What changes can you see coming along in the next year or two?'*

➤

Springboard zone

'Thank you so much – this has been enormously helpful. You mentioned live streaming of events, and that really interests me. Where can I find out more about that?'

This is the stage when you're seeking a springboard moment, an assisted leap to begin a conversation with someone new.

Follow-up questions: 'If you were in my shoes, where would you look next?' 'What organisations are doing exciting things?' 'Who should I talk to?'

Connecting statement: 'I hate ringing people cold. Could you do me a huge favour and email ahead to let your colleague know why this conversation would be helpful to me?'

The springboard method

Springboard conversations add to your knowledge, expand your network and show you how jobs feel from the inside. Use the scripted questions until you develop your own.

There are tough ways of persuading people to see you. You could try working through the Yellow Pages. You could turn up at reception and ask for a meeting. Either might work, but it's much less effort to begin with people who are easy to approach. Start with **three people**. You know them well; they are easy to talk to. They might simply give you encouragement, information or answers to some of your career questions.

Can't think of anyone to talk to? Are you just avoiding the first step? Even people who never think about networking usually have about 100 people within their immediate contact circle. If you're feeling a little more confident, reach out to people you have some connection with through social media.

Ask for a soft handover

Practise with easy contacts, develop your script and ask for introductions to new contacts so you never have to make a cold call. You might say at the beginning: 'I'm hoping to speak to a few people in this sector.' Later, when you say, 'I'm really interested in what you said about X. Who else could I talk to about that?', a name will probably come up.

If you've got names, you've done half the job, because you still have to cold call. Ask for a *soft handover*: 'Do me a favour. I hate ringing people cold. Would you kindly email ahead and say why I'm interested?' A set-up like this means that your next contact expects your call and knows what it's about. The next person knows you're not selling anything, not a time waster and not after a 'big ask'. You only need mention the person who introduced you to get the conversation started.

'What about *you*?'

Be ready for the conversation to flip: *What about you? – what are you looking for?* You don't have to give a full work history, and you don't need to deliver a glib 'elevator pitch'. Briefly mention one thing about your work background, then talk about what's fascinating you at the moment – and what you've discovered through other conversations.

Try a **two-breath message**. On average, you take 15,000 breaths every day. With just two breaths you can say something simple and upbeat:

> **'I'd love to be in a role that allows me to do A and B and C . . . in an organisation that's doing X and Y and Z.'**

A, B and C are your motivated skills (see Chapter 6). X, Y and Z describe things about an organisation that matter to you. You might mention products, services, technology or approaches. You might talk about style (for example, hi-tech or cutting edge), culture (high quality or customer-focused), or the nature of the organisation (private, public, blue-chip, privately owned, etc.). So, for example:

'I'd love to be in a role that that allows me to work with luxury brands and build on my interest in the overall customer experience – in an organisation focused on VIP travel and experiences, or designer products.'

The two-breath message might remind you of the TV show *Ready Steady Cook*: You empty a bag of ingredients and ask someone to make a meal. Responding to this message, people say things like, 'That's interesting. . . have you thought about. . .', suggesting interesting sectors, organisations and people. A warm introduction may be just one more breath away.

Practise your two-breath message so that it flows and feels authentic. It's succinct, unusual and memorable – and gets better results than asking about job openings. It contains ideas others will repeat if your name comes up in conversation. (You can find a more developed version in Exercise 4.2 – Getting your story in focus.)

Follow-up

Many clients assume the best thing to do after a springboard conversation is to send a CV. Remember, a CV is a big ask. If you want to remind someone of your key areas of interest, summarise them in a brief email. A short message is often acted upon immediately; a complicated request gets put to one side.

One superb follow-up is an old-fashioned 'thank you' card. Yes – a real card with a nice picture on the front, sent through the post to an office address. Say thank you, briefly outline how the conversation was useful to you and what happened as a result. A card expresses gratitude with more care and attention than an email, and that's appreciated. Quality cards are hard to throw away, and often remain on a notice board or under the glass of someone's desk for years (include your contact email discreetly on the card so you're easy to find if the card is picked up again).

Don't send further requests for help unless you really need to. It's better if *you* send something helpful – an article, a useful web link or an introduction to someone else.

What if I am invited to consider a job?

Don't ask about specific job openings because that undermines everything you've said about the purpose of the meeting. If a specific role comes up, show curiosity. If it's clear that you're a potential candidate, say you'd like a day or two to prepare for a proper interview. Ask for full details of the job and plan thoroughly, matching your strengths to the key requirements of the job, even if you are in a shortlist of one.

Following the maze

It's easy to feel sceptical about information interviews. People ask, 'How many will I need?' It's hard to predict in advance how many conversations you will need, or which will give the biggest result. It's like working your way through a maze. The treasure could be around the next corner or deep in the maze. You have to trust and keep searching. With persistence, there is magic and surprise in the process – the next conversation could just be helpfully informative, or it could change your life.

Things will happen along the way. You will meet people who will help you at future career turning points, and you will make new friends. You will have fascinating conversations and meet some very interesting people. Thank them for whatever they provide, even if it's just encouragement.

Three predictions

Prediction one: You already know at least one person who can *really* help. When we begin networking, we scan the far horizon for strangers or people we know vaguely. Often there are brilliant people close by – the kind of people you can phone without having to plan what you're going to say.

Prediction two: Whatever job search methods you use, *you'll probably find a job through someone you know already, or someone you meet in the next three months*. Play the game backwards (see Exercise 14.2). Who are you going to call first?

Prediction three is about breakthroughs. Those who teach information interviewing at expert level argue that the best results come from the 'third circle'. You start with people you know, and they introduce you to second circle contacts, who you may know vaguely. The third circle is largely people you don't know at all, and this group gives you the best feedback because they see you objectively. They also offer the most useful leads, because they project you into worlds you know nothing about.

Who can you reach?

Networking for softies means starting with people you already know, but it's useful to know where you want conversations to take you. Think of this in terms of answers to questions. What sectors or roles do you want to know more about? Against each question, write a name. Someone who works in a relevant sector. Someone who used to work in that sector. Someone who knows people in a wide range of occupations. If you get lots of names, that's great, but you only need two or three to start using the 'connections game' resource outlined below.

Exercise 13.1
The connections game

- -

As you investigate sectors and ask great questions, names of organisations will come up. Your personal research will add new names. Work towards a list of target organisations. List them on a spreadsheet.

Organisation name	Contact person	Telephone/ Email	Score/10	Next step

In column 4 give each organisation a score. A score of 1 means you know nothing about the organisation apart from its name. A midrange score means you know how the organisation operates, its style and culture and the kind of roles they regularly fill. A score of 9 means you have met at least two people inside the organisation and 10 means you are talking to someone capable of making you a job offer.

Your goal is to improve each score by at least one point every week. Column 5 records your planned next step. Build connections; reach out to people via LinkedIn or your personal network and keep asking for warm handovers. Keep a note of the name and contact number of people you are trying to reach. Have the list to hand in case someone calls you. Set a diary reminder of follow-up actions agreed.

- -

Jess, working in marketing

Recent graduates often face a dilemma of needing experience for entry-level roles that, particularly in industries where internships tend to be unpaid or ad hoc, can be difficult to obtain without connections. This was Jess's situation when she graduated – trying to break into a competitive industry while struggling to establish any kind of professional network.

Jess writes: 'What I learned about information interviews proved invaluable. It was a novel idea for me that I could feel empowered to contact someone, for instance via LinkedIn or an alumni network, and simply ask to chat about their career.'

It was the emphasis on asking questions and gathering industry insights that really helped – 'I had thought of "networking" as something a bit disingenuous and only for the very confident. The idea of an information interview demystified the process for me, as all I needed was my genuine interest in understanding someone's role and journey. I also discovered that people are really open to discussing their careers!'

'I continue to use information interviews even now, whether I come across a role internally that I want to understand better, or an external company I am wondering about. They transformed my job search and approach to my career, and it always feels like a full circle moment when I am asked for one myself.'

chapter 14

The 4-hour job search programme

'My thinking is first and last and always
for the sake of my doing.'

William James (1890)

This chapter helps you to

- avoid rookie mistakes and understand what will extend a job search;
- monitor your market readiness;
- get tangible results in just 4 hours;
- develop a multichannel job search strategy;
- think backwards about steps to success.

Your condensed, 240-minute programme

This book is designed to take you through a process of change leading to a well-planned, multistrategy job search. Career coaching aims at getting you the right job at the right time. Early results matter, especially in terms of keeping confidence levels high.

It's easy to go to the market too soon. You may spend a lot of time in unproductive activity. You may send out misleading messages. However, there may be reasons you want to get quick results. You might feel you should 'get out there' and apply for roles, recognising that inactivity is getting you down. Family members might be pressuring you to do more. Your savings might be running down. You might fall across an opportunity with a short shelf life.

What can you achieve in 240 minutes? More than you think. You can quickly put your shop window in order, improve your evidence and key messages and learn strategies designed to shorten your job search. You can make the most of technology to reach people who are not available for in-person meetings. And you can avoid classic, obvious mistakes.

Why do smart people make rookie mistakes?

No matter what technology becomes available, we keep making the same basic mistakes when job searching. Looking for a job looks deceptively simple, so we don't focus on what's really required; even experienced candidates make it up as they go along.

Candidates offer indifferent CVs or fail to tailor them to opportunities. They email them out, untested, to all their contacts (look again at your 'default' mode in Exercise 1.1). Others apply for jobs online and, because they receive no response, rehash their CVs or go for lower status roles. Some talk themselves out of the job in the first minutes of their first interview, never understanding what the organisation is looking for.

Don't spend three months recovering from mistakes you make in week one. Make the best of your early energy and your confidence window (see Chapter 2). Don't set yourself up to fail by putting yourself into situations where negative results are guaranteed – for example, applying for attractive roles in competition with hundreds of other people without being really clear about your key messages, or going to recruitment agencies with little idea about the kind of role you're seeking.

Activities likely to make your job hunt LONGER

These are things you might be doing right now which extend your job search:

- Relying solely on the internet to find jobs
- Pursuing only advertised positions in competition with hundreds of other applicants

- Applying for jobs you don't really want 'just for the experience' (and being flattened by rejection)
- Applying for exciting jobs at first and then 'lowering your sights' when things go wrong
- Using up all your best contacts in the first three weeks and then complaining because you don't know anybody
- Networking without knowing why you're doing it or what you want to say
- Spending too much time looking at screens, and not enough time with people
- Approaching senior contacts with a vague request for help and advice rather than specific requests
- Chasing jobs in declining sectors (rather than seeking out the sectors and organisations that are experiencing growth)
- Submitting a CV full of clichés, empty claims and little solid evidence of achievement
- Getting in front of hirers without practising how to talk about yourself
- Going to interviews unprepared, hoping to 'wing it'.

How closely does this list describe what you've been doing recently? Now we turn to activities which will give you a better return on time invested.

Activities likely to make your job hunt SHORTER

Here are methods to help you achieve positive results in the shortest timescale:

- Getting feedback on your CV before sharing it with decision makers
- Rehearsing what you plan to say about your skills, experience and reasons for job change

- Using social media to research people and organisations, and build new relationships

- Having an effective 'shop window' on LinkedIn

- Moving away from email and towards face-to-face conversations

- Networking of any kind – even just talking to friends and neighbours about job ideas

- Conducting information interviews (see Chapter 13) so you get under the skin of target sectors and understand what they're looking for

- Using your best contacts at the right time – approaching senior people only when you're clear how they can help, and you can give them two or three reasons why they should recommend you

- Telling everyone you know what you're looking for, keeping your message focused and simple.

Market readiness

Recruitment consultants talk about 'market readiness' – a state of preparedness that means you're ready to make the most of opportunities and you can safely be put in front of decision makers. How do you know if you're market ready?

Exercise 14.1
Testing your market readiness

Questions	Your answers
Why are you on the market right now? *Danger areas:* talking negatively about why you left your last job, or sounding desperate to get a new role	

➤

Questions	Your answers
What are you? *Danger areas:* trying to cover too many options, or sending out conflicting messages about your main work role	
What are you looking for? *Danger areas:* sounding like you lack confidence, or are hesitant about your next steps	
What are you good at? *Danger areas:* not being prepared to talk concisely (but authentically) about your strengths, with examples ready for interview	
What makes you stand out from other candidates? *Danger areas:* sounding overconfident but unclear about the demands of the job, or uncertain about what you have to offer	

- -

A 240-minute job search in 7 steps

To work through this book takes a day or two. Readers enjoy reflecting, but sometimes want to get results quickly. There are results you can achieve in four hours. Here's a simple programme to help you do just that.

Step 1 – Look at your launch platform

Are you set for blast off? When someone asks, 'Why are you on the market right now?', how much do you reveal about disappointment and uncertainty? Look again at your 'market readiness' and anything that gets in the way. Work out (with the help of others) what you need to do so you're ready for Step 2.

Plan how you will use your time. What job search strategies will you use? What information do you need? Half an hour's planning now will make a big difference. Work out how close you are to a working CV (this isn't just about cataloguing your experience, but matching your evidence to fit target roles).

Step 2 – Get active

One way to misinterpret this book is to think it's purely about self-examination. You need to look out as well as look in. Don't pretend you can only act when everything is ready – the perfect CV, the well-stocked contact book. Don't wait until you can make flawless job applications. And don't wait until people have time to meet you face to face if you want a conversation quickly. It's important not to throw yourself into job hunting unthinkingly, but it's easy to delay. Good enough is fine, perfect gets in the way.

Begin by reaching out to people who will encourage you and remind you what you're good at. Who can keep your spirits up and keep you on track?

Think about gathering information and ideas. Who can you talk to and still be experimental and tentative about your direction? Tap into other people's knowledge, finding out more about work sectors.

You can begin an active search by spending just 45 minutes in online research and a couple of phone calls. Arrange a couple of springboard conversations (see Chapter 13) to deepen your understanding of sectors and improve your visibility.

Step 3 – Get used to talking about yourself

Knowing your skills isn't enough – you need to get this evidence across. The key to fast-paced job hunting is in some ways simple: knowing what your message is, and how to make it stick. Many job hunters are floored the first time someone asks, 'Why should we consider you for this role?'

Practise talking about yourself – particularly your strengths and areas of uncertainty – before sitting in the spotlight. This will make you more focused and less nervous in the first round of interviews. If you find talking about yourself difficult, remember that you will get better through *repetition* (tricking your brain into thinking this is routine, familiar territory rather than a minefield) and *technique*. Spend at least 30 minutes practising out loud – and preparing for tough questions. Talk through your work history with a friend. How do you talk about the high points? How do you talk about your best skills without sounding egotistical or inauthentic?

Work out how to organise your material so you can get key messages across quickly. Communicate why you are on the market at the moment, but also your career story as a whole to make sense of your skills and experience. For difficult issues, prepare safety zone responses (see Chapter 15).

Step 4 – Be clearer about what you're looking for

How do you achieve this clarity? That's a fair question which this book aims to tackle. However, in job search mode, saying 'I'm not really sure what I'm looking for' tends to put the handbrake on. Note that this step is about being *clearer* – not having one single answer – so you can talk about what excites you. Talk about key ingredients in your next role – use the two-breath message (see p. 179).

For rapid results, focus more on the possible rather than the improbable. What doors are likely to open for you quickest? Name organisations, even if you are just using them as examples. Write down a target list of organisations you'd like to approach. Focus on actual job titles that might come up. Develop an action-focused target list (see Exercise 13.1).

Use the list below to focus on the ingredients most likely to get you shortlisted.

Role clues to help if you want to be shortlisted quickly

- The role makes sense in terms of your background, skills and knowledge.
- You can match 4 or 5 key job requirements with bullet points setting out your evidence in a cover email.
- You have around 70 per cent of the requirements of the job description.
- There is something you can offer which makes you worth interviewing – sector experience, special knowledge, managing people or systems, or just adaptability.
- The job will stretch you, even if only marginally. It makes sense as the next entry on your CV.
- The organisation is keen to make an appointment soon, and you can contact a decision maker.

Step 5 – Feature your best self

Organise information about *you*. Your 'best self' isn't a fake version of you, but you at your most impactful. It takes practice (and feedback) to get ready to tell that story.

This book shows you how to catalogue your skills and talk about your strengths, working style and achievements. Make a list of projects you have completed during your career and measurable achievements you're proud of. Find evidence to back up claims about skills and knowledge. Catalogue your material and choose your best material for page 1 of your CV.

Prepare now for demanding questions, e.g. *What makes you stand out from other candidates?* Spend at least one hour before every interview planning for tough questions like this. For each role, offer your *best-matched self*. Focus on the top items an employer is seeking, aligning them with strong pieces of evidence from your history (see Chapter 15 on interviews).

Take 30 minutes to organise your raw material so that you have the first 50 words of your CV or LinkedIn profile. Decide on the key messages you will share with others as you explore and connect.

Step 6 – Get ready to launch

Benchmark yourself against jobs. Use the internet to research the names of jobs you hope to chase, and the skills and qualities they're looking for. Match your evidence, especially in terms of skill level and the language you use to describe what you're good at.

Ask someone with hiring experience to give your CV a 'cold read' (ideally someone who doesn't know your work history). Ask this person to grill you with questions based on jobs you're applying for, and to give you feedback on what you communicate well, and less well.

Market-test material as you develop it – get advice from people who interpret candidate information all the time. Organise your LinkedIn shop window. Does your profile say *what* you are – and summarise key skills? Is it up to date? Look at any work history gaps in your CV, and also credibility gaps in terms of your experience, your qualifications – craft safety zone responses (see Chapter 15) to manage risk.

Step 7 – Search smart

To get quicker results, engage in multichannel job searching. Research work sectors, and start a list of target organisations. Scrutinise job advertisements to identify likely employers and useful agencies. Talk to recruitment consultants who regularly advertise jobs in your target sectors. Approach companies in your chosen sectors on a speculative basis. Write a cover email matching the employer's needs against five six of your key areas of experience.

There are many channels which will take you closer to jobs – recruitment agencies, social media, direct approaches to organisations, job sites, company websites, headhunting and word-of-mouth recruiting. Candidates often rely on just one or two channels, and many rely only on online job boards. This is rather like deciding that whatever your health problem, your only remedy is aspirin. Don't ignore the online world – just give it the time it deserves. Be visible on social media; use LinkedIn to reach out to informative contacts (see Chapter 12).

Today's job market is complicated, with lots of distractions and dead ends, with shifting recruitment strategies from employers. To succeed, you need to operate using all channels, not just the channels you prefer. Combining job search methods increases their power and unlocks the hidden job market. What do you prioritise? Anything that gets you in the room with a decision maker or closer to an organisation with an identifiable need. Spend your time and energy wisely; focus most on activities that shorten your job search and protect your confidence level.

Exercise 14.2
Rewind the video

- -

Imagine that you've found a job you enjoy. One that feels worth doing, engages you and uses your best skills.

Start by thinking what makes the job stimulating. Then rewind – what was the step that got you the job offer? What was the step before that? Work your way back to the first thing you did.

End result	You've been offered a stimulating job that uses your best skills. Write down three or four key features of this job that make it fulfilling. Skills? Knowledge? Context of the job?

➤

Step 6	What did you do to get the job offer? Write down one skill or achievement you highlighted which led to a job offer.
Step 5	What did you do to get shortlisted? Write down two key areas of experience you highlighted to receive the offer of an interview.
Step 4	What did you do to discover that the job exists? List one action you took which helped you know that the role was available.
Step 3	Before discovering the role, how did you discover the organisation? List one action you took to find the organisation.

Step 2	What did you do to find out about the work sector?
	List one action you took to discover and explore the sector.

Step 1	What did you do to start exploring?
	Write down the first thing you did to begin exploring possibilities for career change.

- -

Exercise 14.2 helps if you're feeling you're not making great progress, and also shows you key stages, leading back to where you are now – and the actions you might take in the next day or two. What's the easiest thing to try first? Step 4 above may encourage you to find out more about the hidden job market (see Chapter 12).

Mark, transformation expert

Reflecting on four months of job searching, Mark writes: 'It's felt like a rollercoaster and like fumbling around in the dark.' Mark was feeling both disappointment and confusion: 'I'm starting to wonder if I have a fixed idea about how to find a job.'

Mark's first coaching conversation was rather like taking his car to the garage and plugging it into a diagnostic computer.

➤

The focus is on what's working well, what isn't and where power is being used with little effect.

Deconstructing Mark's job search strategy revealed that he was getting results by making direct approaches to organisations, and networking conversations had felt initially productive. The problem was that each approach ended with a 'we'll let you know if something suitable comes up', and the door had closed.

The first breakthrough for Mark was understanding that he needed a shorter, focused answer to the question, 'What are you looking for?', allowing him to mention the breadth of his experience and what he's really good at.

The next step was filtering the extensive details in his CV and thinking about key messages. The coaching questions 'Why would somebody recommend you?' and 'What are you the go-to person for?' offered useful, concise material.

chapter 15

Getting better results at interview

'Take nothing on its looks; take
everything on evidence.
There's no better rule.'

Charles Dickens (1860)

This chapter helps you to

- rethink interview anxiety and interview preparation;
- anticipate tough questions;
- plan for online interview and selection processes;
- improve the way you get evidence across;
- analyse a job offer and negotiate your starting pay.

How we pretend to prepare for interviews

Everyone takes interviews seriously, but not everybody prepares well. Professional interviewers regularly see candidates who have not planned for basic questions. They expect the interviewer to do the work, dragging evidence out of them, or they hope to 'wing it'. Why do otherwise savvy people leave so much to chance? Probably because interviews are stressful experiences we would rather not think about in advance.

Interview nerves

Anxiety has a positive side to it – adrenalin sharpens the mind. It can also get in the way of what you say. Don't beat yourself up if you experience stage fright – a bone-dry mouth or shaking hands. You can't conquer interview nerves overnight, but you can take immediate steps to reduce their impact. For example, if nervousness makes you clumsy, don't accept a drink if it's offered and have only the briefest paperwork with you at interview.

Nerves can also result in a blank mind and failing to remember great CV evidence. This is where preparation counts. Good planning means you won't pull material out of the air; your evidence will already be matched, in advance, point by point.

One good way of avoiding interview preparation is to pretend that all questions are random and unpredictable. The reality is that around 80 per cent of interview questions can be predicted – yes, four out of five. Most are big, obvious topics related to job content, and easy to spot from job documents. Planning to improvise – rather than prepare – means planning to experience uncontrolled stress.

Exercise 15.1
Employer shopping list

- -

Look at a job description for a role that interests you. Draw a line down the middle of an A4 sheet of paper. In the left column write down, point by point, everything the employer is looking for: qualifications, experience, knowledge, personality attributes. Record everything described as 'essential'. This is the employer shopping list. What is listed first? What seems important? What questions are definitely coming up?

In the right-hand column, write down bullet points that will remind you of your matching evidence – achievements or key experiences – so you can develop short stories (see Chapter 6 on skills and achievements).

- -

Working in the right room

Interviews look like hard work. *Do less work in the interview room.* This doesn't mean being laid back (although being more relaxed helps). If you work hard at anticipating questions and practising stories, you'll have done all the work in your living room, not the interview room. Anticipate surface-level questions relating to the job description, and then dig deeper. Talk to people who know the organisation; find out how success is described. Now think: What demanding questions might *you* be asked? Where do you need to sharpen up your evidence?

The human brain is troubled by the unfamiliar. Repetition tricks your brain into thinking it has done something before, so it seems routine. Rehearse stories so they are concise, energised and focused on what somebody needs. Having preprocessed stories at your fingertips means you can listen to interview questions more carefully and work harder at building relationships in the room.

If time is really short, use a simple formula: **six plus three**. Match stories against the **six** items in the job description you think are most important, and then get **three** additional points across about why you're well matched to the role. This is especially useful in initial screening interviews, which are a quick check that you match essential criteria.

First moments

You're being assessed from the first time you are seen by the organisation, on screen or in person. Dress one notch smarter than the normal dress code for the organisation. For an in-person interview, leave your coat and bag in reception – create the impression that you already work there. You might think that there are a thousand ways to shine in these opening moments, but there are just two:

1 Move calmly to your seat and *keep still.*

2 When invited to say something, be easy to talk to, even if you're just chatting about traffic or the weather.

Opening interview moments are like a *screen test* – a recording of an actor delivering just a few lines. Do you look and sound like you fit the part? Speak clearly, and not too fast. Signal reassurance at every level – you fit in, you can do the job and hiring you won't look like an embarrassing mistake.

Improving your performance

How can you improve your interview skills? If you ask for feedback after an interview, you will probably receive a bland corporate statement about other candidates having more experience than you. (Tip: You sometimes get useful feedback if you ask, 'Can you tell me one thing I can do to improve my interview technique?')

More reliable feedback comes from practice interviews with colleagues who have experience of hiring. Prepare as if it's the real thing, using a real job description. Use the phrasing you plan to use rather than a vague summary ('I'll probably talk about . . . '). At the end of the practice interview, ask for objective information – what was clear or unclear? What messages landed securely? Where did you introduce material that might worry a recruiter?

Friends advise, 'Just be yourself', but that doesn't help very much. Better advice might be: 'Show the interviewer *what you're like on a good day* – the best version of you.' Don't try to 'fake it'. False confidence and fictional claims are fairly transparent to interviewers.

Short stories

Interview time is expensive, so play by the house rules. Let the interviewer set the pace and the agenda – be easy to talk to, and don't hold the floor with over-lengthy answers. You might hope that if you talk for long enough you'll land a good point. However, long answers frustrate the process, creating a risk that the interviewer can't get through the full list of planned questions. Also, interviewer attention usually wanders off after a couple of minutes, so your evidence may not be hitting the mark.

Plan to tell *short* stories. Material becomes easier to remember and easier to listen to. People like stories, particularly if they are entertaining, attention grabbing or just interesting. We remember stories much longer than information, and we remember energised stories longer than ordinary stories.

For every employer need, plan a mini-narrative. Know the exact words you will use to start ('Let me give you an example of where I've done that . . . ') and make sure the middle doesn't go on too long. End by talking about something you changed or something you learned. The first time you present a story, ask, 'Does that give you what you need?' – you should hear if the interviewer wants more detail or if you've missed the point.

Keep stories tight and interesting, around two minutes long. Don't try to learn them word for word, but know how to begin and end each one comfortably. Use a simple structure – for example, identify a problem, explain how you dealt with it and talk about the final result.

Half-prepared candidates 'think about' answers but don't really know how they will begin. Fully prepared candidates know the exact words they will use to launch a story. They have prepackaged answers to tricky questions and know how to land their best evidence. Great stories add sparkle to your answers, drawing on the 'bottled' energy discussed in Chapter 3. Make each story sound fresh (don't repeat phrases from your CV). Rehearse stories aloud at least three times, recording yourself using Zoom or Teams. Listen carefully, but also watch a recording with the sound off to see what your body language says.

Exercise 15.2
The politician's trick

- -

Listen to a politician being interviewed on the radio. No matter what questions are asked, the minister tries to make two or three points about government policy. The questions just provide an opportunity to air a small handful of messages.

You can use the same technique:

- Step 1: 'What three key points about my experience do I want to make during this interview?'

- Step 2: Rehearse them so you can express them in a clear, concise way.

- Step 3: Make sure you get these three points across. If one or two remain unsaid at the end, ask, 'May I just add a couple of points we haven't covered?'

- -

Online interviews and automated selection processes

The world of selecting people is changing, fast. Fewer interviews take place face to face, and more screening happens online.

How do you prepare for an online interview? Dress as smartly as you would for a meeting, but check out how you appear on camera. Look critically at what is in shot around and behind you. Declutter and make the space seem calm and businesslike.

Zoom interviews seem informal, so it's easy to take your eye off the ball. Prepare as for any interview: good stories and attention to job requirements. Sit with key documents in front of you, and make sure that you are uninterrupted. Don't check your phone or try to deal with some other task on your desk or device – give the interview full attention.

The process can easily feel cold and technical, so be easy to talk to. Body language is visible, but your voice does most of the work – sound enthusiastic; vary the volume, pace and pitch. Answer questions slightly more slowly than normal speech, and be concise – it's easy for an interviewer's attention to be distracted. Remember that eye contact is vital, and only happens when you look at the camera, not at a face on screen. Record practice answers so you see what the interviewer sees.

Technology is developing fast, and more interview processes will involve software as well as people. For some years candidates have been asked questions on camera without someone real on the other end of the call. Their recorded answers to standard questions are reviewed separately. Questions might be provided in advance, or might pop up on screen with little notice. Your recorded answers are then compared with other applicants. You might also be asked to give a short presentation to camera, again with no live audience. If you ever have to talk to a machine this way, anticipate questions very carefully, and research examples where other people have faced similar selection processes.

Some automated systems seek typed answers to questions, rather like an online chat system. AI is fast creating the ability to interpret as well as store your answers, and then to pose supplementary or probing questions. Analysis is then passed on to the next stage of a selection process, and candidates who don't cover the basics are screened out. Key terms are clearly vital.

Soon similar processes will use spoken questions and voice recognition to record and interpret answers, so what you say will be analysed instantly by intelligent systems. Answering these questions will probably require a slightly different performance to the one you'd use with a live interviewer, with more careful phrasing. Within the next decade most first-level interviews will probably involve some kind of AI system, and will require new strategies. Again, learning from the experiences of others and finding practice opportunities will be vital.

Preparing for off-the-shelf questions

Interviewers sometimes produce novel questions, but usually ask job-focused 'textbook' questions, including the following:

'**Tell us about yourself.**' This is a deceptively simple opening question. An employer wants to press on, so will be frustrated if your answer is lengthy. Don't unpack your entire work history. Offer a quick overview of the shape of your career, your key skills, and what interests you most in work.

'**What are you most proud of in your working life?**' Practise talking about career high points which show you are motivated and can add value in a role – e.g. times you rescued a situation, delighted a customer, or handled a difficult project.

'**What motivates you?**' Talk about the skills you enjoy using and what you hope to learn. Stress the benefits to the organisation. Show rather than tell – don't just say you are committed and energised – provide examples.

'**Tell me about your strengths and weaknesses.**' Talk about two or three strengths required by the job – with good examples ready to hand. Don't be tempted to discuss things you really believe to be weaknesses – talk about one skill or area of knowledge you'd like to develop (e.g. 'I know I can learn a lot more about ways of measuring customer loyalty').

'**Are you a team player?**' Provide examples of what you've contributed to a team and where you've enabled a team to work more effectively.

'**How quickly will you get up to speed?**' Employers want people who can hit the deck running. Show you learn fast – talk about times you got on top of a challenge quickly and organised your own learning.

'**How do you respond to pressure?**' Give examples of times when you have met difficult deadlines or handled tricky people, kept your cool and got the right result.

'**Why should we offer you this job?**' Show how you have an interesting combination of skills and knowledge, matching them to two or three headline job requirements.

Safety zone responses

What questions do you dread? If you're getting into dangerous territory, it helps to plan answers which feel 'safe' – short, upbeat answers which keep you firmly in your safety zone.

Be brief – this prevents you from getting bogged down in a difficult topic. Staying upbeat avoids dropping negative information into the conversation. A simple structure moves from past to future. For example, dealing with redundancy: 'Like a lot of people, I was laid off when the organisation restructured, but it's given me a chance to focus on what I really want to do . . . '.

Work on safety zone responses for questions you know will be tricky. For really slippery topics (for example, you dropped out of university), plan a second line of defence to anticipate a probing question.

Interview questions where safety zone responses help

'Why didn't you complete the course?' People drop out of learning programmes all the time – difficult to disguise on a CV. Don't go into detail about why a course didn't work for you. State simply that it wasn't giving you what you needed and you made the decision to try something new.

'What did you like and dislike about your last job?' Likes – make a good match between the things that motivate you in work (for example, people, challenges, new learning) and the key things on offer in this new role. Dislikes – talk about things that frustrated your work performance such as bureaucracy or computer failure rather than talking about individuals.

'How do you respond to criticism?' Employers don't have time for ruffled feathers or workplace squabbles. Treat this question as if it's asking about how you respond to feedback. Give examples of times when you have adjusted your working method or tried new approaches. Don't complain that the criticism was unjustified.

'Why are you on the market right now?' If you were made redundant, mention this briefly, then talk about what you want to do now. If you've been unemployed, emphasise your continuing learning and the range of organisations you have looked at.

'How did you get on with your last manager?' Avoid criticism of past bosses. Everyone's working style is different, so show you don't let personality issues get in the way; give examples of where you have worked with a range of colleagues and bosses. Explain different strategies you have used to communicate with people you found difficult.

'What's been the biggest challenge in your career?' Prepare an example of something where you achieved success (or at least came out fighting). Negative information lingers in the mind of interviewers, so pick a positive story – ideally one that highlights skills that are useful to the hiring organisation.

'Why do you want this job at this stage of your career?'
Employers like to hear career stories that make sense. Show you can do the job, and show how the job on offer is the natural next chapter in your career story.

'You seem to have moved around a bit. . . ' Don't apologise for your CV or suggest that it's a series of random events. If you have changed jobs frequently, talk positively about reasons for change and what you learned at each stage.

'We've seen a lot of talented people. Why should we hire *you*?'
You're unlikely to have one 'killer' feature that puts you ahead of the competition. Describe how your skills, knowledge and experience combine together in a unique way to make you the best person for the job. This is often a good opportunity to shake interviewer beliefs: 'You might assume that I don't have enough experience in this sector. In fact . . . '.

Talking about competencies

Competency-based selection processes require a special kind of preparation. Where competencies are listed, match them point-by-point in your application and then prepare a mini-narrative to address each one at interview. Set the scene briefly, outlining challenges or problems you faced, talk about what you did and the outcome. Be prepared to say what you learned from the experience and what you might do differently next time.

Competency stories will usually feature a mix of skills, underpinning knowledge, working style and your attitude to work. In some panel interviews you may get one shot at an answer, so be careful to cover every part of the named competency. Even with highly structured answers, tell engaging stories. Average candidates generalise ('What I usually do is . . . '). Strong candidates talk about specific experiences.

Your chance to ask questions

The final interview question is often, 'Do you have any questions for us?' Too many candidates politely say, 'Thanks, no, you've covered everything in great detail.' Wrong answer! Interviewers remember the first and last things you say more clearly than anything else. Final questions and remarks offer an opportunity to create a lasting impression.

Some interview guides try to persuade you to probe at this moment for information about things like culture, to help you decide if you want the job. This is wrong headed. Questions like this can easily suggest doubt. An interview is about securing a job offer. Decide whether you want the job by undertaking research outside the interview room. The purpose of your final questions is *message reinforcement*, not information gathering – a final positive impression signalling your interest in the role. Prepare three great questions (ask only two – have one spare in case a topic is addressed earlier in the interview).

Before you ask a question, say something positive about the role. Then your question sounds like a buying signal: You like the job so much you want to know more. Don't waste the interviewer's time by asking basic questions answered on the organisation's website. Ask about the future of the job: What learning opportunities are on offer? How will the job develop? Ask about results – how they will be measured, and what do you need to achieve in the first six months? These questions demonstrate strong interest and help the interviewer *imagine you doing the job*. Once an interviewer sees that picture, it's hard to shake.

Interviews with recruitment consultants

Recruitment consultants are professional selectors who earn a living filling vacancies for employers (see Chapter 12). They don't make the final selection decision, but usually decide who to shortlist.

Their credibility depends on presenting employable candidates, so they want to feel you can do the job and will present well at interview. Therefore it's likely that a recruitment consultant will give you useful feedback on your interview strategies and answers, dress code and your market value. If they put you forward for a senior role, they should be able to help you anticipate questions. At other times the external recruiter is hired to perform the first interview. If they grill you about your suitability for a role, that's useful preparation for a conversation with the employer.

Questions to ask yourself when reviewing a job offer

What will this role add to my CV? How will it help me present myself to a recruiter in five years' time? What will I learn in this job?

What parts of the offer do I want to negotiate? Think about the range of things you might want to push back on – money (see below), flexible working, leave, relocation or travel packages, start date, even job content. Only try to change one or two points, otherwise it sounds as if you are being difficult. Never renegotiate something you've previously agreed – this is seen as unprofessional and the whole deal might collapse.

What's the working culture like? Don't ask, find out. While the formalities of a written offer are being completed, ask around. You might even ask to spend a couple of hours with the team you will be joining. This confirms your strong interest in the job, but might help to check if you will fit in. If the organisation turns down your request, you might wonder what's in store.

Do I understand why I am being hired? If you're unsure what skills you offer which seem useful, you probably don't understand the role sufficiently – seek more information before acceptance.

Should I try to influence role content? You won't have the same leverage for at least another 18 months or so of taking the job, so if you feel there is any possibility that you can tweak the job description so that it suits you better, try including this as part of the 'deal'.

What does success look like? Clarity about what's expected of you and what problems you're expected to solve can help enormously with the first 90 days of the job. Ask about preferred outcomes and what's expected of you so you don't face unpleasant surprises down the line.

What if this offer doesn't work for me? Keep job hunting until you sign a contract.

Talking money

At any stage in the process you may be asked, 'What kind of money are you looking for?' Try to keep off the topic until the employer is close to a job offer, when you have maximum leverage.

Any pay request should be based on market knowledge. Find out the pay range that applies to the role, and what evidence you need to offer to get into the top 20 per cent of that range. Don't indicate a salary expectation way above or way below an employer's likely target zone. Saying 'I'm being interviewed for jobs paying between £xxx and £xxx' often sets expectations well. When negotiating, emphasise the value you will add and the size of the problems you will solve.

If the salary offer is too low, take some time to think about your next step. You might come back and ask for a better offer, or you might choose to renegotiate some other part of the job such as flexible working, or areas of responsibility.

Sarah, in-house lawyer

An experienced lawyer, Sarah sought coaching to prepare for a demanding interview for Head of Legal in a large organisation.

'It all felt way outside my comfort zone', Sarah reflected. 'I think quickly as a lawyer, but this situation, answering under pressure, felt very artificial.'

Sarah found it helpful to discover something enjoyable about preparing a presentation to senior staff. She also prepared for the interview in a way she had never done before, starting with a blank piece of paper to list likely questions, and recording matching evidence.

Sarah adds: 'I learned to practise answers to keep them short and focused, and learned how to gain some thinking time when faced with a really difficult question. It's always possible to ask for clarification, summarise the question in your own way, or even give yourself a few extra seconds by offering a couple of different directions that the answer might take. I also learned an authentic way of talking about areas of development rather than weaknesses!'

'What also really worked for me was recording practice answers on video; it was enlightening to see how bored I looked, and also how I smiled or used self-deprecating humour in a way which may seem apologetic rather than well-equipped for the role.'

'And it worked – I got the job.'

chapter 16

Bringing ideas together

'What work I have done I have done
because it has been play. If it had been
work I shouldn't have done it.'

Mark Twain (1905)

The **ideas grid** allows you to see the key ingredients in your ideal career on one sheet of paper. You can find a copy of this ideas grid at http://go.pearson.com/uk/business.

Completing and using the ideas grid

1 Transfer results from the relevant chapters and exercises.

2 Make a copy before you write anything in the Target Sectors box.

3 On one copy, write down any ideas you can come up with for Target Sectors.

4 Show the other, incomplete copy to trusted friends. Ask the question, 'What sectors should I be exploring?' Write down their suggestions.

5 Review your ideas grid frequently (try keeping a copy on the fridge door). Every time you look at it you will probably see new ideas and connections.

6 Change your ideas grid as new information or insights come to light.

7 Turn the document into activity. Your goal is to come up with four target sectors to investigate, and then begin your enquiries. Pick up the phone and talk to someone who is easy to approach.

Exercise 16.1
Ideas grid

My 4 top skills (Chapter 6)

1

2

3

4

My top 4 achievements (evidence vault, Chapter 6)

1

2

3

4

My 2 strongest work themes (Chapter 4):

1

2

My most important values (Chapter 8)

Subjects and sectors that fascinate me (Chapters 7 and 9)

Target Sectors – sectors I plan to investigate

1

2

3

4

Mary Wilson, musician and coach

Looking for a fresh start after advisory work, then bringing up children, Mary wanted new career ideas, wanting to focus on what really mattered – and what she might do next. 'I felt I was drowning in a sea of creative ideas and didn't know which direction to follow.'

The breakthrough for Mary was collating the results of coaching exercises: 'What really motivates, interests, and puts petrol in my engine is surprisingly similar today as it was then. Each year I look back at that ideas grid on a flipchart sheet – summarising my values, interests, and skills – and find they still have an enduring quality: I realised I didn't have to choose between psychology and music but could make links between them in a portfolio career. I learned that my key strength is taking a fusion of concepts/ideas/sounds into a forum where I am out there, being radiant, full of warmth and empathy with a box of delights at my fingertips.'

Years on from this transition Mary writes: 'I'm still coaching, running music groups for babies and toddlers and singing with the band – but also composing music, poetry and been involved in an oral history project on the London folk club scene in the 1950s/1960s. Recently I interviewed a 102 year old which was fascinating!'

Bibliography

Bershin, J. (2019) Let's stop talking about soft skills: They're PowerSkills. https://joshbersin.com/2019/10/lets-stop-talking-about-soft-skills-theyre-power-skills/ (accessed 24 April, 2023).

British Psychological Society. (2017) Psychological testing: A test user's guide. Available online: https://www.bps.org.uk/node/9357 (accessed 18 April, 2023).

Chesterton, G. K. (1905) *Heretics*. London: John Lane, p. 16.

CIPD. (2019) UK working lives: The CIPD job quality index. Available online: www.cipd.co.uk/Images/uk-working-lives-summary-2019-v1_tcm18-58584.pdf (accessed 29 January, 2020).

Csikszentmihalyi, M. (2008) *Flow: The Psychology of Optimal Experience*. Harper Perennial Modern Classics.

de Jong, T., Wiezer, N., de Weerd, M., Nielsen, K., Mattila-Holappa, P. and Mockałło, Z. (2016) The impact of restructuring on employee well-being: A systematic review of longitudinal studies. *Work & Stress*, Vol. 30, No. 1, 91–114.

Department for Education. (2017) Employer perspectives survey 2016. Available online: www.gov.uk/government/publications/employer-perspectives-survey-2016 (accessed 24 April, 2023).

Dickens, C. (1860) *Great Expectations*. Ware: Wordsworth Editions (1992), p. 285.

Dickinson, E. (1863) *Poems of Emily Dickinson*. Boston, MA: Roberts Brothers, 'Poem 670', p. 203.

Edwards, B. (1979) *Drawing on the Right Side of the Brain*. New York: Penguin Putnam.

Emerson, R. W. (1840) *Essays: First Series*. Boston, MA: Phillips, Sampson & Company, p. 53.

Ferguson, M. (1987) *The Aquarian Conspiracy: Personal and Social Transformation in the 1980s*. New York: J.P. Tarcher, p. 112.

Fox, M. (1994) *The Reinvention of Work*. San Francisco, CA: Harper Collins, p. 33.

Frost, R. (1914a) 'The death of the hired man', *North of Boston*. New York: Henry Holt & Co., p. 14.

Frost, R. (1914b) 'The self-seeker', *North of Boston*. New York: Henry Holt & Co., p. 61.

Guare, J. (1990) *Six Degrees of Separation*. New York: Knopf Doubleday Publishing Group.

Herrick, R. (1648) 'Seeke and find', *Hesperides, or the Works Both Humane and Divine of Robert Herrick Esq*, Vol. 2. Boston, MA: Little, Brown & Company (1856), p. 159.

Ibarra, H. (2003) *Working Identity: Unconventional Strategies for Reinventing Your Career*. Cambridge, MA: Harvard Business Review Press.

James, W. (1890) *The Principles of Psychology*. New York: Henry Holt & Co., p. 333.

Jerome, J. K. (1889) *Three Men in a Boat*. Ware: Wordsworth Classics (1993), p. 117.

Kipling, R. (1910) 'If', *Rewards and Fairies*. New York: Doubleday, Page & Company, p. 175.

Krucoff, C. (1984) The 6 o'clock scholar: Librarian of Congress Daniel Boorstin and his love affair with books. *The Washington Post*, 29 January, 1984, p. K8.

Lawrence, D. H. (1928) 'Work', reprinted in *The Complete Poems of D.H. Lawrence*. London: Heinemann (1972), p. 450.

Layard, R. (2005) *Happiness: Lessons from a New Science*. London: Penguin Books.

Lees, J. (2012) *The Interview Expert – Get the Job You Want*. London: Pearson Education.

Lees, J. (2013) *Just the Job! – Smart and Fast Strategies to Get the Perfect Job*. London: Pearson Education.

Lees, J. (2013) *Knockout CV*. Maidenhead: McGraw-Hill Education.

Lees, J. (2017) *Knockout Interview* (4th ed.). London: McGraw-Hill Education.

Lees, J. (2017) *The Success Code*. London: John Murray Learning.

Lees, J. (2020) *Get Ahead in Your New Job*. London: McGraw-Hill Education.

Mental Health Foundation (2021) *Work–Life Balance*. Available online: https://www.mentalhealth.org.uk/a-to-z/w/work-life-balance (accessed 24 April, 2023).

O'Connor, S. (2015) I quit! Job resignations and the UK labour puzzle, *The Financial Times*, 25 March, 2015. Available online: https://www.ft.com/content/632649cf-fffe-3926-bde0-9e4497d7e01d (accessed 18 April, 2023).

Pink, D. (2009) *Drive: The Surprising Truth About What Motivates Us*. New York: Riverhead Books.

Pryor, R. and Bright, J. (2011) *The Chaos Theory of Careers*. London: Routledge.

Reade, C. (1870) *Put Yourself in His Place*. Boston, MA: Fields, Osgood & Co., p. 21.

Rohr, R. (1999) *Everything Belongs*. New York: The Crossroad Publishing Co., p. 19.

Ruskin, J. (1851) *Pre-Raphaelitism*. New York: John Wiley, p. 7.

Smith, M. (2019) *The Grace-Filled Wilderness*. London: SPCK, p. 76.

Taylor, M. (2017) Good work: The Taylor review of modern working practices. Available online: https://www.gov.uk/government/publications/good-work-the-taylor-review-of-modern-working-practices (accessed 18 April, 2023).

Terkel, S. (1974) *Working: People Talk About What They Do All Day and How They Feel About What They Do*. New York: The New Press, p. xi.

Todd, B. (2014) To find work you love, don't (always) follow your passion. Available online: https://80000hours.org/articles/dont-follow-your-passion/ (accessed 2 May, 2023).

Twain, M. (1905) A humorist's confession, *The New York Times*, 26 November, 1905.

Whitehead, A. N. (1925) *Science and the Modern World*. New York: Macmillan, p. 4.

Wilde, O. (1893) *Lady Windermere's Fan, a Play About a Good Woman*. London: Samuel French, Act 1.

Williams, R. (1995) *A Ray of Darkness: Sermons and Reflections*. Lanham, MD: Cowley Publications, p. 152.

Wiseman, R. (2010) *59 Seconds: Think a Little, Change a Lot*. London: Pan Macmillan.

Index